Censorship

Andrea C. Nakaya, *Book Editor*

Bruce Glassman, *Vice President*
Bonnie Szumski, *Publisher*
Helen Cothran, *Managing Editor*

OPPOSING
VIEWPOINTS®
SERIES

D1469170

GREENHAVEN PRESS
An imprint of Thomson Gale, a part of The Thomson Corporation

THOMSON
─────✦─────™
GALE

Detroit • New York • San Francisco • San Diego • New Haven, Conn.
Waterville, Maine • London • Munich

© 2005 Thomson Gale, a part of The Thomson Corporation.

For more information, contact
Greenhaven Press
27500 Drake Rd.
Farmington Hills, MI 48331-3535
Or you can visit our Internet site at http://www.gale.com

Cover credits: © Photodisc/Photos.com

LIBRARY OF CONGRESS CATALOGING-IN-PUBLICATION DATA

Censorship : opposing viewpoints / Andrea C. Nakaya, book editor.
    p. cm. — (Opposing viewpoints series)
  Includes bibliographical references and index.
  ISBN 0-7377-2925-2 (lib. : alk. paper) — ISBN 0-7377-2926-0 (pbk. : alk. paper)
    1. Censorship—United States. 2. Mass media—Censorship—United States.
  3. Internet—Censorship—United States. 4. Freedom of speech—United States.
  I. Nakaya, Andrea C., 1976– . II. Opposing viewpoints series (Unnumbered)
  Z658.U5C433 2005
  363.31'0973—dc22   2004054309

Printed in the United States of America

"Congress shall make no law...abridging the freedom of speech, or of the press."

First Amendment to the U.S. Constitution

The basic foundation of our democracy is the First Amendment guarantee of freedom of expression. The Opposing Viewpoints Series is dedicated to the concept of this basic freedom and the idea that it is more important to practice it than to enshrine it.

Contents

Chapter 4: Is Freedom in the United States Threatened by Censorship?

Why Consider Opposing Viewpoints?

"The only way in which a human being can make some approach to knowing the whole of a subject is by hearing what can be said about it by persons of every variety of opinion and studying all modes in which it can be looked at by every character of mind. No wise man ever acquired his wisdom in any mode but this."

John Stuart Mill

In our media-intensive culture it is not difficult to find differing opinions. Thousands of newspapers and magazines and dozens of radio and television talk shows resound with differing points of view. The difficulty lies in deciding which opinion to agree with and which "experts" seem the most credible. The more inundated we become with differing opinions and claims, the more essential it is to hone critical reading and thinking skills to evaluate these ideas. Opposing Viewpoints books address this problem directly by presenting stimulating debates that can be used to enhance and teach these skills. The varied opinions contained in each book examine many different aspects of a single issue. While examining these conveniently edited opposing views, readers can develop critical thinking skills such as the ability to compare and contrast authors' credibility, facts, argumentation styles, use of persuasive techniques, and other stylistic tools. In short, the Opposing Viewpoints Series is an ideal way to attain the higher-level thinking and reading skills so essential in a culture of diverse and contradictory opinions.

In addition to providing a tool for critical thinking, Opposing Viewpoints books challenge readers to question their own strongly held opinions and assumptions. Most people form their opinions on the basis of upbringing, peer pressure, and personal, cultural, or professional bias. By reading carefully balanced opposing views, readers must directly confront new ideas as well as the opinions of those with whom they disagree. This is not to simplistically argue that everyone who reads opposing views will—or should— change his or her opinion. Instead, the series enhances readers' understanding of their own views by encouraging confrontation with opposing ideas. Careful examination of others' views can lead to the readers' understanding of the logical inconsistencies in their own opinions, perspective on why they hold an opinion, and the consideration of the possibility that their opinion requires further evaluation.

Evaluating Other Opinions

To ensure that this type of examination occurs, Opposing Viewpoints books present all types of opinions. Prominent spokespeople on different sides of each issue as well as well-known professionals from many disciplines challenge the reader. An additional goal of the series is to provide a forum for other, less known, or even unpopular viewpoints. The opinion of an ordinary person who has had to make the decision to cut off life support from a terminally ill relative, for example, may be just as valuable and provide just as much insight as a medical ethicist's professional opinion. The editors have two additional purposes in including these less known views. One, the editors encourage readers to respect others' opinions—even when not enhanced by professional credibility. It is only by reading or listening to and objectively evaluating others' ideas that one can determine whether they are worthy of consideration. Two, the inclusion of such viewpoints encourages the important critical thinking skill of objectively evaluating an author's credentials and bias. This evaluation will illuminate an author's reasons for taking a particular stance on an issue and will aid in readers' evaluation of the author's ideas.

It is our hope that these books will give readers a deeper understanding of the issues debated and an appreciation of the complexity of even seemingly simple issues when good and honest people disagree. This awareness is particularly important in a democratic society such as ours in which people enter into public debate to determine the common good. Those with whom one disagrees should not be regarded as enemies but rather as people whose views deserve careful examination and may shed light on one's own.

Thomas Jefferson once said that "difference of opinion leads to inquiry, and inquiry to truth." Jefferson, a broadly educated man, argued that "if a nation expects to be ignorant and free . . . it expects what never was and never will be." As individuals and as a nation, it is imperative that we consider the opinions of others and examine them with skill and discernment. The Opposing Viewpoints Series is intended to help readers achieve this goal.

David L. Bender and Bruno Leone,
Founders

Greenhaven Press anthologies primarily consist of previously published material taken from a variety of sources, including periodicals, books, scholarly journals, newspapers, government documents, and position papers from private and public organizations. These original sources are often edited for length and to ensure their accessibility for a young adult audience. The anthology editors also change the original titles of these works in order to clearly present the main thesis of each viewpoint and to explicitly indicate the opinion presented in the viewpoint. These alterations are made in consideration of both the reading and comprehension levels of a young adult audience. Every effort is made to ensure that Greenhaven Press accurately reflects the original intent of the authors included in this anthology.

Introduction

"If we are to allow freedoms at all there will constantly be complaints that either the liberty itself or the way in which it is exercised is being abused. . . . There is no way of having a free society in which there is not abuse. Abuse is the very hallmark of liberty."

—former Lord Chief Justice Halisham

In February 2004 approximately 90 million Americans sat in front of their television sets for the Super Bowl, one of the most-watched TV broadcasts in America. Viewers of all ages were watching as singers Justin Timberlake and Janet Jackson performed in the halftime show, dancing provocatively with one another onstage. Then, in a preplanned stunt, creating a moment that would be remembered in Super Bowl history, Timberlake reached across and ripped off a piece of Jackson's bustier, revealing her bare right breast to toddlers and grandparents alike. The performance prompted shock and outrage from viewers across America, and the Federal Communications Commission (FCC), the government agency responsible for regulating communications in the United States, received thousands of complaints.

This event highlighted and renewed a debate that has been ongoing throughout U.S. history. The First Amendment to the Constitution protects free speech, and the entertainment industry is included in that protection. At the same time, many people believe that some of the content generated by the entertainment industry is extremely offensive and harmful to society, and that a certain amount of censorship is necessary to protect America's children and its culture. Critics continue to disagree over how far the First Amendment protection of free speech should extend when it comes to entertainment that is available to people of all ages.

According to journalists Katy Kelly, Kim Clark, and Linda Kulman, the 2004 halftime show symbolizes the way entertainment content has deteriorated in the United States. They see Jackson's exposure as a manifestation of "the crudity and salaciousness, the violence and easy morality that have so permeated U.S. mass culture that even the Super Bowl, the quintessential family television event, is no longer immune." FCC commissioner Michael J. Copps agrees that entertainment has become increasingly vulgar and offensive to many people. He uses television as an example, arguing that the networks are competing in a "race to the bottom." Commissioner Kevin J. Martin echoes Copps: "Television today contains some of the coarsest and most violent programming ever aired." According to one study, profanity during the family hour on television increased 95 percent from 1998 to 2002. Many other studies show that there is more sexual content on TV than ever before. "At the FCC, we used to receive indecency complaints by the hundreds," says Martin. "Now they come in by the thousands."

It is widely argued that this "race to the bottom" in entertainment is harmful to society. Robert Peters, president of Morality in Media, believes that crude and vulgar entertainment harms Americans. He argues that the deterioration of entertainment will eventually lead to the deterioration of American culture. "When your popular culture begins to undermine everything you think is good in your society, you're headed for trouble," he says. "There's a lot of good in America, and, relatively speaking, not much good makes the news or entertainment media. To me, it's literally a life and death issue for our society."

Many people argue that government censorship is the only way to protect society from harmful entertainment since the entertainment industry is not responsible enough to censor itself. "It appears that some radio and TV broadcasters . . . must be reminded not only of their public interest obligations but also of the critical role they play in forming and shaping society," says FCC commissioner Kathleen Abernathy, who believes that the FCC should regulate entertainment content more strictly. Proponents of censoring the industry argue that the entertainment industry is motivated by profit, not by what is most beneficial for society. "They are not going to do what is right," states Peters.

Freedom of speech, however, is one of the foundations of U.S. society. The right to speak freely has been consistently defended by the U.S. Supreme Court, and any attempt to censor entertainment, even if it is believed to be for the good of society, runs the risk of violating the First Amendment. The FCC has historically protected free speech by leaving entertainment content largely to market forces and free choice. FCC chairman Michael K. Powell backs up the commission's stance by pointing out how important it is to protect all forms of speech, even unpopular ones. "We must use our enforcement tools cautiously," he warns. "Government action in this area can have a potential chilling effect on free speech." Author Marjorie Heins argues that censorship can be dangerous because it means imposing one person's standards on the rest of society. According to her, "History suggests the danger of giving government officials the power to impose their standards of taste or decency on any speech that minors might see or hear. Their judgments are usually conservative, conventional, and dismissive of radical or minority styles."

The debate about censorship in entertainment is especially contentious as it concerns America's children. Legal adviser Patrick Trueman argues that social benefits, including the protection of children, are sometimes more important than absolute support for free speech. "The First Amendment is to benefit everyone," he maintains, "but that's not to say we can't have laws against indecency. . . . [The First Amendment] is a freedom that turns into a slavery if we are no longer allowed to protect our children and instead enslave them in this culture we're developing." In contrast, Professor Robert Thomson insists that while much entertainment content is inappropriate for children, this does not mean it should be censored. He points out that this would necessitate censoring what adults are allowed access to. "If we legislate against anything inappropriate for a child, we may also eliminate good programming for adults," he argues. "Like liquor and toxic cleaning products, some TV content is a potential hazard to children, to be responsibly managed by parents but not necessarily removed by federal fiat."

Entertainment is only one area in which censorship is fiercely debated in the United States. The authors in *Opposing Viewpoints: Censorship* explore a number of other facets of the censorship debate.

CHAPTER 1

Should There Be Limits to Free Speech?

Chapter Preface

In 1993 Holocaust deniers—people who believe the Holocaust never happened—placed an advertisement in a number of college newspapers. The ad falsely claimed that the Holocaust Memorial Museum contains no proof that gas chambers actually existed. Critics charged that the ad was offensive and untrue, and should not have been published. College newspaper editors defended their decision to run the ad by explaining that it was a form of free speech protected by the First Amendment. As places of knowledge and learning, schools and universities are also places where many different forms of expression take place, some of these extremely controversial. As a result, debates about censorship and free speech frequently involve these institutions.

Many people believe that censorship has no place in educational institutions. Kermit L. Hall, president of Utah State University, points out that one of the central roles of schools and universities is promoting freedom of expression. He explains that while free speech on campus may include speech that many people disagree with, freedom is an essential part of learning. According to Hall, "One of the driving concepts of the university campus is academic freedom, the right to inquire broadly, to question and to promote an environment where wrong answers, seemingly absurd ideas and unconventional thought are not just permitted but even encouraged." Columnist David Limbaugh agrees that censorship has no place in an educational institution. He believes that censorship is dangerous because it inevitably privileges a particular point of view while minimizing others. Limbaugh cites campus speech codes as an example of the dangers of school censorship. "Speech codes are merely an excuse to justify censorship," he argues, "Speech codes are tools that administrators use to quash speech they do not agree with, and to punish students and faculty members for expressions they do not agree with."

Not everyone believes in absolute freedom of speech on campus, however. Writer Stephen Hicks maintains that free speech may need to be limited if it interferes with the rights of others. According to Hicks, "Education is a form of communication and association, fairly intimate in some respects, and it requires civility if it is going to work. So open displays of hatred, antagonism, or threats in the classroom or anywhere else in the university undermine the social atmosphere that makes education possible." According to Professor Deborah Tannen, as institutions of knowledge and learning, universities have an enormous influence on society. She believes that universities have a responsibility to protect society by censoring some speech. Tannen claims that, "universities have a responsibility to encourage open debate and discussion of a wide variety of views, but they also have a responsibility not to disseminate false information and lend credibility to those who spread it."

The First Amendment to the U.S. Constitution protects free speech. However, as the debate over censorship on college campuses illustrates, that right often conflicts with other rights in American society. The result is a debate on whether censorship is justified in certain situations, or whether all speech should be free and protected. The authors in the following chapter examine some of these difficult issues.

"The question isn't whether you are for or against it, but how much censorship you want and where you want it."

Limits Must Be Imposed on Free Speech

Jonah Goldberg

Censorship is necessary and occurs every day in many facets of our society, asserts Jonah Goldberg in the following viewpoint. According to Goldberg, the most important question concerning censorship is not whether it should be used, but how. He criticizes censorship trends in the United States, arguing that Americans have mistakenly fought to protect many minor freedoms, such as the right to produce offensive artwork, while censoring more important things, such as democratic debate, that should not be restricted. Goldberg is editor-at-large of *National Review Online*, a conservative journal of opinion. He also writes a nationally syndicated column, which appears in a number of newspapers, including the *Philadelphia Inquirer*, the *Washington Times*, and the *San Francisco Chronicle*.

As you read, consider the following questions:
1. What are some examples of censorship that commonly occur in the United States, as cited by Goldberg?
2. What, specifically, was the First Amendment intended to protect, according to the author?
3. Why does Goldberg argue that "stealth advertising" be allowed?

Jonah Goldberg, "Free Speech Rots from the Inside Out," *The American Enterprise*, vol. 14, January/February 2003, p. 52. Copyright © 2003 by The American Enterprise Institute for Public Policy Research. Reproduced by permission of *The American Enterprise*, a magazine of Politics, Business, and Culture. On the Web at www.TAEmag.com.

There's a TV commercial currently [in 2003] running in Washington, D.C., and, for all I know, nationally. It features a bunch of young hipsters using everyday trash as musical instruments. "Never throw away anything you can use to express yourself!" says the voiceover. That pretty well sums up the state of today's culture.

This fetishization of free expression also shows up in the white-knuckled phobia of censorship that has permeated our media and institutions. From the American Library Association's insistence that every branch library must allow unfettered access to Internet pornography, to the propagandistic "Read a Banned Book" T-shirts sold by activists, to the ponderous newspaper editorials which butcher [pacifist] Martin Niemoeller's "first they came for the Jews" warning[1] every time a museum is criticized for another dung-and-urine desecration of the Virgin Mary,[2] America has convinced itself that we are a hair's breadth away from *Fahrenheit 451*.[3] Among elites, unfettered self-expression is the highest good, and even the most innocuous forms of censorship are presented as evil by definition.

It's understandable that people in the First Amendment business would be protective of their franchise. And, yes, free expression is good and nice and important. But, the entire culture, particularly the media, has been brainwashed to believe that censorship is always and everywhere a threat to our very freedom. When I tell college audiences that I favor censorship, the gasps of shock from liberal and conservative students alike nearly suck in the walls and pull the ceiling down.

Some Censorship Is Inevitable

I ask these kids "Do you think ABC should be allowed to run triple-X porn on Saturday morning?" Well, if you say no, then you believe in censorship. Similarly if you think strip clubs can be zoned, kiddie-porn banned, and copyright laws

1. This warning, about the failure of Germans to speak out against Nazi crimes against Jews during World War II, has been used to illustrate the dangers of censorship. 2. In 1999 a painting of the Virgin Mary embellished with elephant dung was displayed in the Brooklyn Museum of Art in New York City. Many people were offended by the exhibit and this sparked controversy over whether some artworks should be censored. 3. a 1953 novel about a world where books are banned and critical thought is discouraged

enforced, you support censorship. (Copyright laws are one of the oldest forms of censorship: They bar people from disseminating someone else's work without permission. Try to release a movie starring Mickey Mouse or Snoopy and you'll see how quickly a court orders you to stop.) And, once we establish that you support some censorship, the question isn't whether you are for or against it, but how much censorship you want and where you want it.

American Attitudes About the First Amendment

The First Amendment became part of the U.S. Constitution more than 200 years ago. This is what it says: "Congress shall make no law respecting an establishment of religion, or prohibiting the free exercise thereof; or abridging the freedom of speech, or of the press; or the right of the people peaceably to assemble, and to petition the Government for a redress of grievances." Based on your own feelings about the First Amendment, please tell me whether you agree or disagree with the following statement: *The First Amendment goes too far in the rights it guarantees.*

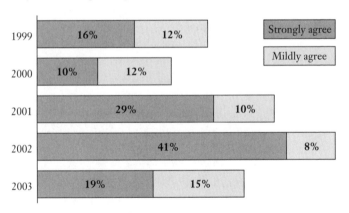

"State of the First Amendment 2003," www.firstamendmentcenter.org.

The fact is that the Founding Fathers were not "against" censorship. The First Amendment is a prohibition against the federal government restricting a free press. Few if any of the Founders would be troubled by obscenity laws. The problem today is that the First Amendment has been thoroughly butchered, with editorialists at the *New York Times* swinging some of the biggest cleavers.

Consider these editorial positions which reflect the general schizophrenia regarding free expression and censorship. The *New York Times* is in favor of the federal government forcing tobacco companies to pay for speech that is directly inimical to their interests. But when the Clinton administration wanted to reward TV networks for running anti-drug messages, the *Times* declared: "In allowing government to shape or even to be consulted on content in return for financial rewards, the networks are crossing a dangerous line they should not cross. On the far side of that line lies the possibility of censorship and state-sponsored propaganda."

Calling Censorship Something Else

Censorship today is simply defined as censorship we don't like. Censorship we do like is "responsible policy." This kind of thinking is a cancer on the very idea of free speech. The *Times* (and the *Washington Post*, the *Los Angeles Times*, et al.) favors campaign finance laws which sharply regulate the only speech the Founders considered sacrosanct—political speech. Today, anonymous political speech is called "stealth advertising" and the *Times* wants it banned. The *Federalist Papers*[4] were anonymous. Tom Paine's *Common Sense*[5] would have to be filed with the FEC [Federal Election Commission] today. Yet while the big media companies (and the Democrats) claim that such draconian regulations are vital to the existence of the republic, they champion an absolutist right of free expression in matters of culture. Cuts in subsidies for "performance art" or feces smeared on canvas are seen as, gasp, "censorship" by a bunch of fascistic prudes.

Americans generally protect fringe freedoms in order to keep core freedoms safe. But here we treat the fringe as the core and the core as the fringe. Vile obscenity is a testament to the beauty of free expression, but free democratic debate is to be censored. Free speech in America is rotting from the inside out.

---

4. a series of articles about the U.S. Constitution published between 1787 and 1788
5. an influential pamphlet published in 1776 that advocated American independence

"Freedom of expression . . . is 'the matrix, the indispensable condition of nearly every other form of freedom.' Without it, other fundamental rights . . . would wither and die."

Free Speech Must Be Protected

American Civil Liberties Union

It is vitally important that Americans continually fight to protect free speech, argues the American Civil Liberties Union (ACLU) in the following viewpoint, because without free speech, democracy is impossible. According to the ACLU, even unpopular expression, such as hate speech, must be protected in order to preserve the freedom that the First Amendment gives to all Americans. The ACLU is a nonprofit organization dedicated to preserving liberty in the United States.

As you read, consider the following questions:
1. Even if speech is antithetical to the very freedom the First Amendment stands for, why must it be protected, according to the ACLU?
2. Why did John Stuart Mill believe that all ideas must be represented in society?
3. How does free speech give the American people a "checking function," as argued by the ACLU?

American Civil Liberties Union, "Freedom of Expression," www.aclu.com, February 27, 2002. Copyright © 2002 by the American Civil Liberties Union. Reproduced by permission.

Freedom of speech, of the press, of association, of assembly and petition—this set of guarantees, protected by the First Amendment, comprises what we refer to as freedom of expression. The Supreme Court has written that this freedom is "the matrix, the indispensable condition of nearly every other form of freedom." Without it, other fundamental rights, like the right to vote, would wither and die.

But in spite of its "preferred position" in our constitutional hierarchy, the nation's commitment to freedom of expression has been tested over and over again. Especially during times of national stress, like war abroad or social upheaval at home, people exercising their First Amendment rights have been censored, fined, even jailed. Those with unpopular political ideas have always borne the brunt of government repression. It was during WWI—hardly ancient history—that a person could be jailed just for giving out anti-war leaflets. Out of those early cases, modern First Amendment law evolved. Many struggles and many cases later, [the United States] is the most speech-protective country in the world.

The path to freedom was long and arduous. It took nearly 200 years to establish firm constitutional limits on the government's power to punish "seditious" and "subversive" speech. Many people suffered along the way, such as labor leader Eugene V. Debs, who was sentenced to 10 years in prison under the Espionage Act just for telling a rally of peaceful workers to realize they were "fit for something better than slavery and cannon fodder." Or Sidney Street, jailed in 1969 for burning an American flag on a Harlem street corner to protest the shooting of civil rights figure James Meredith. . . .

Free speech rights still need constant, vigilant protection. New questions arise and old ones return. Should flag burning be a crime? What about government or private censorship of works of art that touch on sensitive issues like religion or sexuality? Should the Internet be subject to any form of government control? What about punishing college students who espouse racist or sexist opinions? In answering these questions, the history and the core values of the First Amendment should be our guide. . . .

What Does "Protected Speech" Include?

First Amendment protection is not limited to "pure speech"—books, newspapers, leaflets, and rallies. It also protects "symbolic speech"—nonverbal expression whose purpose is to communicate ideas. In its 1969 decision in *Tinker v. Des Moines*, the Court recognized the right of public school students to wear black armbands in protest of the Vietnam War. In 1989 (*Texas v. Johnson*) and again in 1990 (*U.S. v. Eichman*), the Court struck down government bans on "flag desecration." Other examples of protected symbolic speech include works of art, T-shirt slogans, political buttons, music lyrics and theatrical performances. . . .

Asay. © by Charles Asay. Reproduced by permission.

The ACLU [American Civil Liberties Union] has often been at the center of controversy for defending the free speech rights of groups that spew hate, such as the Ku Klux Klan and the Nazis. But if only popular ideas were protected, we wouldn't need a First Amendment. History teaches that the first target of government repression is never the last. If we do not come to the defense of the free speech rights of the most unpopular among us, even if their views are antithetical to the very freedom the First Amendment stands for, then no one's liberty will be secure. In that sense, all First Amendment rights are "indivisible."

[Censoring so-called hate speech also runs counter to the long-term interests of the most frequent victims of hate: racial, ethnic, religious and sexual minorities. We should not give the government the power to decide which opinions are hateful, for history has taught us that government is more apt to use this power to prosecute minorities than to protect them. As one federal judge has put it, tolerating hateful speech is "the best protection we have against any Nazi-type regime in this country."] . .

Three Reasons Why Freedom of Expression Is Essential to a Free Society

It's the foundation of self-fulfillment. The right to express one's thoughts and to communicate freely with others affirms the dignity and worth of each and every member of society, and allows each individual to realize his or her full human potential. Thus, freedom of expression is an end in itself—and as such, deserves society's greatest protection.

It's vital to the attainment and advancement of knowledge, and the search for the truth. The eminent 19th-century writer and civil libertarian, John Stuart Mill, contended that enlightened judgment is possible only if one considers all facts and ideas, from whatever source, and tests one's own conclusions against opposing views. Therefore, all points of view—even those that are "bad" or socially harmful—should be represented in society's "marketplace of ideas."

It's necessary to our system of self-government and gives the American people a "checking function" against government excess and corruption. If the American people are to be the masters of their fate and of their elected government, they must be well-informed and have access to all information, ideas and points of view. Mass ignorance is a breeding ground for oppression and tyranny.

"Any negative effects free expression has on children affect not only children but society as a whole."

Censorship Should Be Used for the Protection of Children

Kevin W. Saunders

Children should not have the same First Amendment rights as adults, argues Kevin W. Saunders in the following viewpoint. While the First Amendment protects adult free expression from government regulation, children need to be protected from some material, such as violent or sexual media content, he contends. Thus, he maintains, the government is justified in imposing limits on what children can be exposed to. According to Saunders, these limits are necessary in order to teach children good values. Saunders is a professor at Michigan State University College of Law and author of *Violence as Obscenity: Limiting the Media's First Amendment Protection.*

As you read, consider the following questions:

1. Why does the author believe that the U.S. government is failing in its duty to society and coming generations?
2. What is paternalism, according to Saunders?
3. As cited by the author, why is it necessary for children to wait until adulthood to enjoy full individual rights?

Kevin W. Saunders, "Should Children Have First Amendment Rights?" *The Responsive Community*, vol. 13, Summer 2003, pp. 12–22. Copyright © 2003 by *The Responsive Community*. Reproduced by permission.

In 1949, Justice [Robert H.] Jackson wrote: "There is danger that, if the Court does not temper its doctrinaire logic with a little practical wisdom, it will convert the constitutional Bill of Rights into a suicide pact." Similarly, writing for the Court in 1963, Justice [Arthur J.] Goldberg stated: "While the Constitution protects against invasions of individual rights, it is not a suicide pact." The position that the Constitution is not a suicide pact finds support in other opinions of the Supreme Court and lower courts.

Yet, how better for a society to commit suicide than to fail in its duty to raise its youth in a safe and psychologically healthy manner? We are so failing. While rates fluctuate, violent crime by youth is unacceptably high. Homicide is the second leading cause of death for 15- to 24-year-olds and the leading cause among African-American males of that age. Teenage pregnancy rates are also too high. Although down 11 percent from its 1994 high, the birth rate for unwed 15- to 19-year-olds was 41.5 births per thousand in 1998. Children also use tobacco and alcohol at unacceptable rates. The Campaign for Tobacco Free Kids cites government reports showing that more than 4 million 12- to 17-year-olds are current smokers, and 48.2 percent of high school boys used tobacco in the month preceding a 1997 survey. The Campaign for Alcohol Free Kids reports that 10 million American teenagers drink monthly; that 8 million drink weekly, a half million of those binge drinking; that alcohol consumption is not uncommon at ages 11 and 12; and that a majority of grade five through twelve students say that advertising encourages them to drink. We are failing in our duty to society and its coming generations, and the First Amendment's limitations on our ability to restrict the influences children face are among the roots of that failure.

Children Need Protection

The First Amendment does contain the most important of our political freedoms. Stating those freedoms very succinctly, the amendment says: "Congress shall make no law respecting an establishment of religion, or prohibiting the free exercise thereof; or abridging the freedom of speech, or of the press; or the right of the people peaceably to assemble, and to petition the government for a redress of grievances." The importance of the amendment for adults is obvious, but its importance for children is less clear. Even if children should enjoy some First Amendment rights, the benefits those rights provide may well be limited by a child's developmental state. Rather than conclude that the rights of children and adults should be equal, the possibility of limiting children's right to correspond to children's capacities should be considered.

Free expression also has its costs. While there are limitations on adult expression, those limitations are narrow. Only when a clear and present danger attends the speech or when the speech falls within certain categories—obscenity, fighting words, or libel—may adult speech be limited. When the recipient of the speech is a child still developing psychologically, the costs of unrestrained speech may be too high. Shielding children from harm adults may have to tolerate protects children in their development. This same shielding also serves to protect the rest of society. Any negative effects free expression has on children affect not only children but society as a whole.

The thesis of this article is that the First Amendment should function differently for children and for adults. For communication among adults, the amendment should be fully robust, perhaps even more so than under current law. Where children are concerned, however, the amendment should be significantly weaker. Society should be allowed to limit the access of children to materials not suitable to their age. Most people might be surprised to learn that the two-tiered approach to the First Amendment that I am proposing would generally be considered a departure from existing interpretations; at the moment, courts make it very difficult to limit the access of children to violent materials, vulgar or profane materials, and the hate-filled music used to recruit the next generation to supremacist organizations. Legal prohibitions on distributing sexual materials to children are now [in 2003] constitutional, and my approach would extend this treatment to the materials listed above. No good reason requires that we recognize a right on the part of children to such access. Nor should the free expression rights of adults be seen as including a right to express themselves to the children of others. The full development and autonomy of adults may require the right to express themselves on a wide variety of topics, but that right should not include access to children not their own. Perhaps no one should tell authors, producers, or computer programmers what they can create. But that is not the same as saying that they have a right to juvenile audience for their books, films, or video games.

Antipaternalistic Feeling

Those who argue for strong individual rights or autonomy consider the imposition of morality through the law illegitimate, but it is important to understand the nature of the objections. However complex or sophisticated the way in which the argument is presented, it seems to come down to the complaint that society's attempt to enforce morality is paternalistic. That is, when the state forbids behavior that only affects consenting, competent participants, the only basis for the intervention is the state's belief that it knows better than the individual what is best for that individual. There are, of course, contingent arguments over who is affected by the behavior, but the jurisprudential issue is over the right of the state to limit the individual's ability to make decisions having an effect solely on that individual.

When the charge of paternalism is raised against a proscription regarding adult behavior, it has some impact. Clearly, it would further the individual's own best health interests if the state were to forbid smoking. But our society believes that individuals should be able to make their own decisions in such cases. The same applies to the use of alcohol, although drug laws seem to indicate the limits of the culture's receptiveness to such autonomy arguments.

When it comes to issues of free expression, the antipaternalistic feeling is particularly strong. Through the first half of the 20th century, adult use of obscene materials was routinely suppressed, largely on the theory that such use was not good for the individual. While obscenity laws continue to exist, their enforcement has become more lax and the likelihood that a particular work will be found obscene has decreased. The decreasing acceptability of paternalism was central in *Stanley v. Georgia*. In that case, the Supreme Court reversed a conviction for the possession of obscene materials in the privacy of the defendant's home. The state argued that it had the right to protect the mind of the individual from the effect of obscenity, but the Court flatly rejected the claim, concluding that "if the First Amendment means anything, it means that a State has no business telling a man, sitting alone in his own house, what books he may read or what films he may watch." The Court went on to say that the state "cannot constitutionally premise legislation on the desirability of controlling a person's private thoughts."

Censoring Television to Protect Children

When the founding fathers conceived [the right to freedom of speech], I think it's safe to assume that they hadn't imagined their innocent children watching the "devil boxes" that TV's have become. Imagine if they had been shown a clip from [the movie] "Die Hard", with [actor] Bruce Willis toting an Uzi [machine gun], mercilessly killing hundreds of men. Is that freedom of speech? Perhaps, but we need to ask ourselves if this type of free speech is either appropriate, or acceptable for a person of any age. The resounding answer is no. Should children . . . be watching a program where people are being murdered? Is murder amusement? If it is, consider the ill state that our society must be in the depths of.

Frank Patriot, "Protect the Children," www.enduringvision.com.

Since many arguments against restrictions on free expression, like many arguments against the enforcement of morality generally, are based on antipaternalistic feelings, it is important to understand just what is wrong with paternalism. Paternalism, when it is wrong, is wrong because it is an affront to equality. When the state tells the individual what is in the individual's best interest, the state discounts the individual's own view as to how to balance his or her own interests. It treats the individual as less able to make such a decision than the majority the state represents, and numbers alone should not resolve such disagreements over individual goods.

Paternalism Is Appropriate for Children

Children, however, are not equals in this regard. Knowing what one's best interests are requires an ability to make judgments that children, depending on their age, may completely lack or that may be insufficiently developed in them. "Paternalism" means acting like a father. That may be inappropriate when the action is toward an adult, but it is completely appropriate when a father or mother acts that way toward his or her child. Children need to be taught how to act, both when the acts involved may have an effect on others and when the issue is what is in the child's own best interests. The same is true when the issue is what to read or see. There may be no right to interfere with an adult's decisions as to the materials he or she believes contribute to understanding or happiness. With children, however, it is appropriate for parents to decide what materials run counter to their child becoming the sort of person they think the child should be and to refuse to allow the child access to those materials.

The state also serves a role with regard to children that is, in a sense, parental. . . . The role of the state, so long as the parents are not unfit, is secondary to the parents, but just as preventing non-parents from selling tobacco to minors is not objectionably paternalistic, limiting the ability of non-parents to distribute harmful media to children should not be objectionably paternalistic.

Promoting Good Values

Allowing the state to limit third party expression to children would enable society to promote good values without imposing majority views on or limiting the personal autonomy of adults. The community would have the period of the child's minority to transmit its values from generation to generation. This fits with [philosopher] John Stuart Mill's own recognition that society has the period of childhood to teach its children how to act. At the same time, once a child reaches adulthood, individual rights can come into full bloom. Such individual rights may still interfere with or run counter to community values, but the community had its opportunity to teach those values. If it has failed to do so, the values may simply be of insufficient strength to override the commitment to individual rights society also recognizes.

Society may have a right to make people morally better, but it has the period of minority to do so. Children must be trained, morally as well as in other areas. They need to be made into the morally best people they can be, but the project should be relatively complete by the time the child reaches the age of majority. To carry it on beyond that age is disrespectful of the equality of the individual. To engage in the task before the age of majority is to recognize that children are, in fact, not equals, in a sense, and that they need help in their development. The acceptance of a strong First Amendment for adults and a weaker First Amendment for children would allow society to protect children's best interests as well as its own.

Violence and the First Amendment

The distribution of violent material such as videos and video games illustrates why the dual approach to the First Amendment makes sense. *Doom* is the best known of the "first-person shooter" genre of video games. In these games the player holds a realistic hand gun and fires at people who pop up or come around corners on the video screen. Killing quickly and efficiently produces high scores. The games are such good training that adaptations are used by the armed forces and law enforcement agencies. Most users, however, are not soldiers but teenage boys.

In 1997, Michael Carneal was a 14-year-old freshman at Heath High School in Paducah, Kentucky. He enjoyed playing *Doom* and similar video games. He had also seen the film *The Basketball Diaries*, in which the film's hero, in a dream sequence, goes to school with a firearm under his trench coat and guns down a teacher and several classmates. One morning Carneal went to his school with a stolen pistol, arriving just as a prayer group was breaking up. He opened fire on the group and with nine shots inflicted head or chest wounds on eight students, killing three. He did so with no firearm experience other than on video games.

Two years later, Eric Harris and Dylan Klebold went to Columbine High School in Littleton, Colorado. They were heavily armed, and by the time they were finished and committed suicide, they had killed a teacher and 12 students and had wounded 23 others. They too were avid *Doom* players. One had given his sawed-off shotgun the name of a character from the game. They also appear to have been influenced by *The Basketball Diaries*, going so far as to adopt the dress of the film. . . .

Recognizing the difference between the free expression interests of adults and children only makes sense. The dual approach would be in the best interests of children and society.

"Acting on fear and suspicion and assumption, we have, with the best of intentions, created situations that are potentially more harmful to kids and teens than what we want to protect them from."

Censorship Is Not an Effective Way to Protect Children

Charles Taylor

Society should not censor free expression in order to protect children, asserts Charles Taylor in the following viewpoint. There is no proof that exposure to images of sex and violence harms children, contends Taylor. Further, he argues, protecting children from these images may actually be dangerous since it leaves them ill-prepared to experience real life when they become adults. Charles Taylor's essays on popular culture have appeared in a number of publications including *Details*, *Newsday*, the *New Yorker*, and *Spin*.

As you read, consider the following questions:
1. As argued by Taylor, what is wrong with the data that Congress uses to back up its support for censorship?
2. Who should take responsibility for deciding what is and is not appropriate for children, according to the author?
3. What is the problem with movie ratings, as cited by the author?

One of the most unbelievable conversations I've ever had took place a few years ago with a friend, a writer, who was in the midst of preparing for a visit from some relatives, including a young cousin of about 10. My friend told me that he'd gone through his house putting away any "inappropriate" material that his cousin might see. We're not talking porn here, or removing [controversial novelist] Henry Miller or [novel] "The Story of O" from the bookshelves, but stashing the copies of [the magazines] "Esquire" and "Entertainment Weekly" in the magazine pile in his living room. Why, I asked, would you feel the need to hide those? Because, my friend explained, they had swear words in them. I pointed out that the worst thing his cousin was likely to see in "Entertainment Weekly" was, as it's so delicately printed in that magazine, "f——," something the boy had certainly already heard in the schoolyard. But my friend wasn't buying. Why, he wanted to know, can't magazine articles be written so that they're suitable for everyone?

A False Assumption

I felt as if I had been asked to justify why water had to be wet. Here was someone who depended for his living on the right to free speech, who wrote as an adult for other adults, who was advocating the false assumption that lies at the core of the censorious impulse: Children need to be protected from vulgarity and obscenity.

At the heart of that argument is the belief that society should be remade for everyone, not just children. Basically, my friend was arguing that all adult discourse should be rendered suitable for kids, that entertainment or writing specifically intended for adults is somehow dangerous and that, as journalists, we should all be required to adhere to a phony "family newspaper" standard.

He didn't come out and say that, of course. He fell back on the protection-of-innocence arguments that censors have used for years and that courts have upheld. There's an understandable impulse behind the desire to protect children, an awareness of their physical fragility, a wish for them to be able to enjoy their childhood and a frustrating sense that out in the world dangers await them that we are powerless to stop. But too often we have lost the ability to distinguish between what's inappropriate for kids and what is actually harmful to them. And, acting on fear and suspicion and assumption, we have, with the best of intentions, created situations that are potentially more harmful to kids and teens than what we want to protect them from.

Children Do Not Need Extra Protection

The tradition of censorship in the name of the little ones is the subject of Marjorie Heins' new [2001] book, "Not in Front of the Children: 'Indecency,' Censorship, and the Innocence of Youth." Heins, the director of the Free Expression Policy Project at the National Coalition Against Censorship, has essentially written a précis of various legal rulings that have cited the protection of youth as justification for limiting free speech. Heins is blessedly clear on the legal ramifications of the obscenity prosecutions she considers. As a lawyer she's adept at pointing out the contradictions, false premises and just plain unconstitutionality of those decisions. . . .

Heins must have realized she was striding into a minefield. Shrewdly—but also, I think, honestly—she focuses on the harm done to children by censorship laws. She questions how children who have been so stringently shielded can be well prepared for life (especially when at age 18—poof!—they magically become "adults"); how, under the Constitution, some citizens can be judged to have fewer free-speech rights than others; and how you can claim to be protecting children if, in the case of birth control or sexual information, you are depriving them of something that, especially with the public health crisis of AIDS, could save their lives. Some parents love to wag their fingers condescendingly at those of us without children who oppose free-speech restrictions. They say, "You'll change your tune when you have kids of your own." But why would anyone wish for a world in which their children would have *fewer* rights?

The notion that words and images and ideas can cause harm to young minds has become such an article of faith that it's hard not to feel a sense of futility when you point out that there is not a shred, not an iota, not an atom of proof that exposure to images or descriptions of sex and violence does children any harm. In the face of people who are certain about the evil Pied Piper effect of the media, insisting on the facts becomes pointless, even though every expert who tries to claim otherwise gives himself or herself away. On May 6 [2001], the Associated Press reported news of an American Psychiatric Association panel on online voyeurism in which a University of Michigan psychiatry professor named Norman Alessi testified that "the potential of seeing hundreds of thousands of such images during adolescence—*I have no idea what that could do.* But *I can imagine* it must be profound" (emphasis added). God knows psychiatry isn't science, but you'd expect a doctor to be little more circumspect when he has only his imagination to go on.

Yet this is exactly the kind of "data" that Congress swallows whole before coming up with some new way to put the screws to Hollywood. And witnesses who do try to testify to the facts are often treated with contempt. MIT [Massachusetts Institute of Technology] professor Henry Jenkins appeared before the Senate in the hearings that convened in the panicked aftermath of the Columbine killings[1] and found himself to be the only scholar present who didn't take it on faith (because there's no other way to take it) that media violence promotes real violence. Jenkins described a Senate chamber festooned with "hyperbolic and self-parodying" posters and ads for the most violent video games on the market. "Senators," he said, "read them all deadly seriously and with absolute literalness."

The Media Get the Facts Wrong

And why wouldn't they? What do senators, what do the most vocal media critics for that matter, know about video games, rock 'n' roll, current movies and television? [Senator] Joe Lieberman admitted to [television show] "Entertainment Weekly" last week [June 2001] that he hasn't seen a movie since going to "Crouching Tiger, Hidden Dragon" just before the Oscars. Think he had a chance to see many during last

1. In 1999 two students of Columbine High School in Colorado opened fire at the school, killing a teacher and twelve students, and wounding twenty-three others, before committing suicide.

year's [2001] campaign? Think that will keep him from open-ing his yap about the sinister effects of media violence. . . .

I have never come across one—not one—critic protesting the perniciousness of media sex and violence who had any sense of irony, or any substantial or direct experience with the way audiences experience sex and violence and the dif-ferent ways they're portrayed. I know a 16-year-old girl who has seen "The Faculty" [movie] 14 times. Now, I can imag-ine what Lieberman or Henry Hyde would do with that tid-bit—turn it into the story of a teenager obsessed with a movie in which students take up arms against their teachers. The fact is, my friend has seen it repeatedly for the same rea-son she went to an opening night IMAX [movie theater] screening of [movie] "Pearl Harbor": because she thinks [ac-tor] Josh Hartnett is adorable.

Who Decides What Is Harmful for Children?

Who decides precisely what speech is harmful to minors? . . . Our diverse society is deeply divided over questions about sexual morality, race discrimination, militarism, vengeance, and gun ownership. Are minors morally corrupted or ener-gized and informed by rap? We, "as a society," disagree. I doubt that even [author Michael] Massing and I, let alone society, could reach consensus on the ideal media diet for America's youth. . . .

What threatens First Amendment freedoms more than any isolated instance of censorship is the unifying rationale of all censorship campaigns: the presumption that "bad" speech directly causes "bad" behavior and that government officials should be empowered to distinguish good speech from bad.

Michael Massing and Wendy Kaminer, *American Prospect*, January 1–15, 2001.

Why we resist facing the facts in this debate is under-standable. People don't have to be stupid or corrupt to look at school shootings, or violence in America in general, and feel that *something* has to be responsible. And as someone who spends much of his time looking at pop culture, I won't deny being disturbed by some of the more mindless violence out there, of having felt cut off from an audience that was grooving on mayhem. People feel so overwhelmed by vio-lence that they think there simply must be a connection between media bloodshed and the real thing. But the truth is that violent crime is down in America, and it has been going down for some years now.

Just because I think extreme protectionism is misguided doesn't mean that I think children should be exposed to anything and everything. Parents have to make those decisions for their own kids. And while I sympathize with their frustration over the proliferation of outlets like the Internet, video and cable that makes those decisions more demanding, parents' frustration isn't a good enough reason to limit the First Amendment. It sickened me when I heard stories about parents dragging along their young kids to see [horror movie] "Hannibal." But we see that kind of idiocy even with a damaging movie ratings system in place. Teenagers may be better able to handle material than their younger siblings are, but they too are the target of obscenity laws that don't distinguish between a 6- or 8-year-old and a 14- or 16-year-old.

Some will insist that there have been findings indicating a causal link between violent entertainment and violent behavior. But those studies have profound flaws. Is it really that surprising that toddlers become markedly more rambunctious after being kept in a room watching "The Three Stooges" for five hours? I have some faith in science, and it seems to me that if there really were a cause-and-effect link between real violence and media violence, then it would have been proven by now. At the least, people who believe in that link should work the flaws out of their methodology. . . .

Meddling Parents

Nothing attracts kids' curiosity or spurs their resourcefulness faster than what's forbidden to them. Have a shelf of books or videos you've told your kids are for Mommy and Daddy only? I guarantee you they've perused it. And sure, as kids all of us at one time or another came across things that upset us or confused us or gave us nightmares. I had to stop watching [television series] "Rod Serling's Night Gallery" because it gave me insomnia. And I vividly remember the unsettling mixture of queasiness and thrill in the pit of my stomach in elementary school when a classmate brought in some grainy black-and-white porno photos of a woman giving a man a blow job. But do you know anyone who's been done lasting harm by looking at dirty pictures or watching a violent movie who wasn't already emotionally disturbed to begin with? There's a big difference between wanting to screen what your kids are reading or watching—in other words, nudging them toward good stuff to balance the mountain of available crap— and wanting to keep them in a hermetically sealed bubble that admits nothing of the outside world. The latter approach, which is the "good parenting" at the basis of so many government attempts to restrict kids' access to information, is, at root, an insult to kids, a presumption that they are too stupid or fragile to be given information about the real world.

And of course it's a threat to the civil liberties of the rest of us. Perhaps out of an instinct for the politic, Heins doesn't address the arrogance of parents who think that in order to solve their child-rearing problems, the rest of adult society should have key freedoms curtailed. It's time to put the responsibility for deciding what is and isn't appropriate for children squarely on parents.

I know often this is a question of time. I see how hard it is for friends to balance raising kids with the financial necessity of having two working parents. But parents' convenience isn't a good enough argument for measures that narrow the free-speech rights of adults. . . .

Parents Inconvenienced by the First Amendment

And the granddaddy of all nincompooperies, the Motion Picture Association of America ratings system, originally supposed to protect filmmakers from interference, has instead resulted in studios contractually obligating them to cut their films to what's acceptable for a 17-year-old. Otherwise, they can't avail themselves of crucial newspaper and television advertising. (Many outlets won't accept ads for NC-17 [no one under 17 admitted] films.) The ratings have never been constitutionally challenged. There's no telling how the current Supreme Court would rule on the system, though there's no doubt of its unconstitutionality. The courts have consistently ruled that adult discourse cannot be required to be conducted at a level suitable for children.

A few years ago I got into a heated discussion with some

parents over the ratings system. It was startling because it revealed how much some parents believe the rest of us owe them. I argued that ratings should be abolished not only because they were unconstitutional, and have led to de facto censorship, but also because even a cursory glimpse at a review from a critic they trust would give parents better information about the content and tone of a movie. The parents I was talking to seemed outraged that they should have to read a review before deciding whether they would allow their kids to see a movie. Ratings, they insisted—demonstrating that their minds were much more innocent than the ones they were protecting—made sure their kids were only allowed into movies their parents had approved. When I asked why parents couldn't accompany kids to the box office to ensure the same thing, it was as if I had suggested some Herculean task.

I think it's fair to ask how parents who feel that reading a review or driving their kids to a movie theater is too much work ever manage to pull off the greater responsibilities that parenthood entails. What amazed me during this discussion was that the parents seemed completely willing to abandon their responsibility to be informed about the culture their kids were growing up in to some anonymous watchdog. And that willingness makes them much more susceptible to senators who know that calling for decency is always good for political capital, to citizens or religious groups that feel they have the right to make their values the standard for everyone else, to professional witnesses and "experts" who use their degrees and studies the way real-estate swindlers use phony deeds. Sure, it's easier to believe that [movies] "The Matrix" or "The Basketball Diaries" provided blueprints for the Columbine massacre, or that [musician] Eminem is promoting mother raping and homophobia. It's *always* easier not to think.

Stunting Kids Intellectually

But fear and ignorance are never a good basis for making any decision. In the broadest terms, this insistence that children see only material that teaches approved values is a way of stunting kids intellectually. It institutionalizes the [former U.S. secretary of education] William Bennett definition of art as a delivery system for little object lessons on virtue.

I'm not saying that art (and even books and movies that may be less than art) has nothing to teach, but what it does teach is the complex and contradictory nature of experience, experience that resists easy judgments. So by making art abide . by narrow and vague standards of decency, we're making kids ill-equipped not just to experience art but to experience life.

Danger of Keeping Kids Uninformed

And there's a more urgent danger. In the midst of a public health crisis, denying minors access to sexual information is an insane way to "protect" them. Heins cites a 1998 study that puts our teen childbirth rate ahead of all European countries. Even Mexico, a country where the Catholic Church is such a strong presence, offers much more forthright public health information to teens.

By contrast, by the '90s a [conservative activist] Phyllis Schlafly–inspired program called "Sex Respect" had gotten hundreds of thousands of dollars in government grants and was still being taught in one out of eight public schools. "Sex Respect" informed students that the "epidemic" of STDs [sexually transmitted diseases] and teen pregnancy is nature's judgment on the sexually active; that "there's no way to have premarital sex without hurting someone"; that HIV [human immunodeficiency virus] can be contracted through kissing; that premarital sex can lead to shotgun weddings, cervical cancer, poverty, substance abuse, a diminished ability to communicate and death. Heins describes one video in which a student asks an instructor what will happen if he wants to have sex before getting married. The answer: "Well, I guess you'll just have to be prepared to die."

You have to admire the honesty of that response. Because, of course, whether or not they admit it, the people who want to deny teenagers access to sexual information (to say nothing of access to condoms or abortion) are implicitly saying that kids should die rather than have their innocence sullied. It's always a temptation in the culture wars to sound superior, to give in to ridiculing the values and beliefs of others. But some values need to be ridiculed. The people keeping kids in the dark may be articulate and well dressed and prosperous, but the morality they're selling is that of hicks and ignoramuses and yahoos. How many times in the past 80 years has America proved that it hasn't learned one basic lesson: Prohibition doesn't work. The bodies pile up from our war on drugs and still we haven't learned it. How many teenage bodies need to pile up before we apply that lesson to our national preoccupation with decency?

*"The right of the media to information . . .
is subordinate to the right of the American
people to have their armed forces conduct
operations without journalistic disclosure of
sensitive information."*

The Press Should Practice Self-Censorship During Times of Crisis

Carlos A. Kelly

While freedom of the press is an essential part of American democracy, in times of war that need must be balanced with the need to protect sensitive military information, argues Carlos A. Kelly in the following viewpoint. Kelly believes that during war, the First Amendment right to free speech should not be absolute for the media. He contends that secrecy is often important for successful military operations, and thus the media should exercise self-restraint and good judgment about what information they disclose to the public. Kelly is an attorney who specializes in commercial disputes.

As you read, consider the following questions:
1. What two ideals collide when the armed forces and news organizations interact, according to the author?
2. Historically, what two methods have the armed forces used to restrict media access in times of war, as cited by Kelly?
3. According to the author, how did the media inadvertently aid the Iraqis during the Persian Gulf War?

On September 11, 2001, shortly after airplanes struck the Twin Towers [in New York], the media revealed the deployment of the U.S.S. *Theodore Roosevelt*, an aircraft carrier, to New York City. At a time when an identifiable enemy could not be located—when the enemy should have been presumed to be at large—the media disclosed the location of U.S. forces. Since then, some members of the media have complained that their right to report is being unnecessarily abrogated by Pentagon restrictions. For example, journalist Peter Arnett has said he "[doesn't] see why reporters cannot be in the B-52s that are starting to launch continuing air strikes [on Afghanistan]." Commenting on another journalist's observation that government authorities restricted broadcasts of [terrorist leader] Osama bin Laden's image as a precaution against inadvertently transmitting secret signals to other terrorists, Arnett has said "that controlling the message . . . is an overwrought reaction by government authorities." Add to those remarks the view of some that a media consortium should purchase a controlling interest in a reconnaissance satellite in order to ensure the media has access to space-based cameras so that satellite photographs may be available for the use of the media, free of the auspices of government. . . .

Balancing Competing Interests

The implications of exercising control over the media in time of war are significant. The lifeblood of democracy, a form of government that derives its power from the consent of the governed, flows, in part, because of the existence of an informed citizenry. Thus, in time of peace and time of war, in order to maintain the legitimacy of the government, citizens must know what actions are being prosecuted in their name. However, during time of war, limits to this proposition must exist. If the survival of the Republic is at risk, the courts likely will assist the legislative and executive branches when they act to preserve the Republic—even if it means temporarily curtailing, by as limited a means as possible, certain freedoms so that the virtues of liberty can be fully enjoyed as soon as the threat is vanquished. As Americans, we prize our freedoms; this article's proposition recognizes and embraces those freedoms, while arguing that the common sense approach suggested by the Supreme Court . . . in regard to the First Amendment in time of war should trump an unfettered media right of access. As a result, the media should exercise self-restraint and judgment when covering military operations. Such self-restraint would strike a balance between competing interests and achieve a sensible policy of providing citizens with needed information while protecting American lives on the battlefield. Significantly, the media self-restraint proposed in this article, by its very nature, should not signal a general roll-back of civil liberties.

Origins of Conflict Between Media and Armed Forces

Throughout history, the relationship between the armed forces and the media has been marked by disagreement and competing objectives. Sun Tzu, the ancient Chinese warrior and author, counseled commanders that the "formation and procedure used by the military should not be divulged beforehand." One of the U.S. Army's eight principles of war is surprise. In contrast, the purpose of news organizations is to disclose information. Necessarily, the two ideals—secrecy and disclosure—collide when the armed forces and news organizations interact.

Secrecy remains important even after a mission has been accomplished. Allowing the media to publish secret or sensitive information after the "surprise" has been sprung is no solution. The enemy may be able to gain an advantage with the "after-the-fact" information. For example, in World War II, a reporter, after learning Allied Intelligence had broken the Japanese code, published the names of Japanese warships used in the Battle of Midway, which revealed the Allies' ability to crack the code. Fortunately, the Japanese never capitalized on the publication; nevertheless, the magnitude of the potential loss resulting from a Japanese realization that their naval code had been broken illustrates the need for continuing secrecy in particular circumstances.

In order to prevent, or at least control, the disclosure of information, the armed forces have used two primary methods in attempting to restrict the media in time of war. The first method of control is censorship. Military censors delete information, regardless of source, that is deemed unfit for publication. Similarly, the armed forces may review information before publication and ask the media to refrain from publishing what has been deemed to be sensitive information. The second method of control in time of war is more basic—restricting media access to sources of information. Instead of censoring sensitive information, the armed forces prevent the media from acquiring sensitive information. Press pools,[1] restricting physical access from particular areas, misinformation, and the use of preferred correspondents all fall into the category of restricting media access to sensitive information. . . .

Media Access During Persian Gulf War

We now turn to the battlefield application that set the stage for media access in the wake of September 11th: the Persian Gulf War. In the Gulf War, General Norman Schwarzkopf's media policy was based on his experience in Vietnam, especially what he perceived to be a media that harmed U.S. interests. However, Schwarzkopf also believed that an outright ban on the media in the Persian Gulf would be a mistake. . . . Schwarzkopf's fundamental belief about the media was "that our own newspaper and TV reports had become Iraq's best source of military intelligence." (Ultimately, Schwarzkopf was proved correct in his belief that news reports were used by the Iraqis for intelligence purposes.) At one point during the war, Schwarzkopf exclaimed, "This stinks! *Newsweek* just printed our entire battle plan."

Despite Schwarzkopf's skeptical view of the wartime role of the news media, he intervened on behalf of the Western media so that journalists might have access to the theater of operations. For example, in August 1990 the Saudis had decided to ban all journalists from their country, the staging ground for the liberation of Kuwait. The U.S. Central Command, headed by Schwarzkopf, persuaded the Saudis not to implement the journalist ban. Similarly, on the night of February 23–24, 1991, Secretary of Defense Dick Cheney an-

1. a group of reporters who collect information to be shared with other news organizations

nounced a 48 hour news blackout to coincide with the commencement of the ground war against the Iraqis. Schwarzkopf opposed the length of the blackout and gave a press briefing five hours after the ground war began.

American Opinions Regarding Censorship During War

Please tell me whether you agree or disagree with the following statements: "The government should be able to review in advance what journalists report directly from military combat zones."

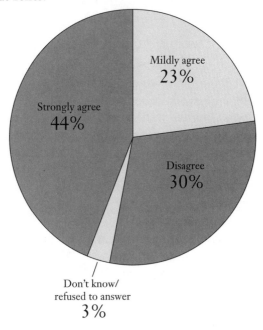

"State of the First Amendment 2003," www.firstamendmentcenter.org.

Outside of the intercessions by Schwarzkopf, media access was strictly limited by the pool system. A Department of Defense publication, the *Desert Storm Ground Rules for Media*, provided a list of rules by which journalists had to abide. The rules "banned publication or broadcast of specific information the department wanted to keep secret, including numbers of troops, aircraft, weapons, equipment and supplies; future plans and operations; locations of forces; and tactics." In addition, all combat reporting would be done in pools that were subject to security review prior to release; no reporters would be allowed free movement within combat zones.

Some elements of the media tried to circumvent the ground rules by heading into the desert in search of a story. A CBS News reporter, Bob Simon, and his news crew were captured by Iraqis. Ironically, CBS requested military force to free Simon and his crew, which unnecessarily placed American forces at risk, even though the journalists' plight was caused by their withdrawal from the pool system.

The Need for Self-Restraint

Journalistic zeal, ordinarily a desired quality of the press, in time of war can be a flaw, which can have far-reaching, and dire, consequences. During the Gulf War, some journalists disclosed sensitive information; other journalists unnecessarily put U.S. forces in harm's way when their overzealous pursuit of a story led to their capture by Iraqi forces. Given these incidents from a previous conflict, and the attitudes of some journalists in the aftermath of September 11th, the need for a sensible media policy based upon the media's exercise of self-restraint becomes clear.

The survey of the case law suggests the conclusion that the right of the media to information from the battlefield, if any right even exists, is subordinate to the right of the American people to have their armed forces conduct operations without journalistic disclosure of sensitive information. While the U.S. wars against terrorism, restricting media access to sensitive information is necessary to protect American lives and is supported historically and jurisprudentially. In order to ensure the existence of the First Amendment for future generations of Americans, a temporary and limited restraint on media access is necessary. Media decision makers—from reporter to publisher—must use common sense and judgment when covering matters military; just because one can publish something does not mean one should. Even the exercise of this broadest of rights—freedom of the press—like freedom of speech is tempered by "the circumstances in which it is done."

> *"A press that is alert, aware and free most vitally serves the basic purpose of the First Amendment. For without an informed and free press there cannot be an enlightened citizenry."*

The Press Should Not Be Censored During Times of Crisis

Anthony Lewis

It is in times of crisis, such as America's war on terrorism, that press freedom of expression is most important, argues Anthony Lewis in the following viewpoint. Lewis believes that the media is an important safeguard of democracy in the United States. Not only should the press have the right to free expression; it is obligated to guard against censorship and keep the public fully informed about domestic and international events, he contends. Lewis, a columnist for the *New York Times* from 1969 to 2001, won the Pulitzer Prize in 1955 and 1963. He is the author of *Make No Law: The Sullivan Case and the First Amendment.*

As you read, consider the following questions:

1. According to Lewis, how has the Bush administration attempted to prevent media criticism of its actions?
2. As cited by the author, why did the media agree to broadcast only short segments of the Osama bin Laden tapes?
3. How did the media show courage during the Vietnam War, according to Lewis?

Anthony Lewis, "Law and Journalism in Times of Crisis," *The Advocate*, vol. 61, November 2003, p. 817. Copyright © 2003 by Anthony Lewis. Reproduced by permission of the author.

L awyers and journalists have an important role in American society—more important, I suppose, than in any
other country. But it is especially important, indeed crucial,
right now. The reason is that we depend on the men and
women of those two professions to keep us free in what is a
hard time for civil liberties. Let me give you an example of
what I mean.

Maher Hawash

Maher Hawash is a naturalized American citizen who works
for the Intel Corporation in Portland, Oregon. A month ago
[in October 2003] he was arrested when he arrived at work.
A dozen armed officers raided his home that same morning,
waking his wife, Lisa, and three children. Since then Mr.
Hawash has been held in solitary confinement. He has not
been told why he is there. The only explanation the U.S.
Justice Department has given is that he is being held as a
"material witness" in an investigation by something called
the Joint Terrorism Task Force.[1]

The federal material witness statute was designed to as-
sure the presence of grand jury witnesses who might flee.
The present attorney general, John Ashcroft,[2] is using it for
quite a different purpose: to detain indefinitely, and interrogate, people he suspects of a connection with terrorism. The
Justice Department tries to keep the detentions under a
blanket of secrecy, and most judges have gone along with
that course. When lawyers went to a federal court on behalf
of Mr. Hawash, the judge put them under a gag order forbidding them to talk about the case.

Does the Hawash case scare you? It scares me. And it
scares friends of Mr. Hawash in Oregon who are trying to
get some explanation from the federal authorities. Steven
McGeady, a former Intel executive, said: "You hear about
this happening in other countries, and to immigrants [here],
and then to American citizens. And finally you hear about it
happening to someone you know. It's scary." I wonder
whether Mr. McGeady was deliberately paraphrasing what

---

1. In February 2004, Hawash was sentenced to seven years in prison for conspiring
to wage war against the United States.   2. Ashcroft resigned in November 2004.

the German pastor Martin Niemoller said about not caring when the Nazis came for the Jews and then for the Communists—not caring until they came for him.

When the press heard about what had happened to Maher Hawash, at the beginning of April [2003], *The New York Times*, *The Boston Globe* and other papers ran a story. I know it is hard to cover something blanketed in secrecy. But I think the practice of jailing Americans in secret demands attention: non-stop attention. *The Times*, to give it due credit, published another story [in November 2003]. Mr. Hawash was still in prison, with no explanation.

The Hawash case is not the only one of its kind. Others are being held under the material witness statute. The pervasive secrecy makes it impossible to know how many; estimates run from 20 to 40. But there is another category of federal detentions that is even more worrying, this one without any basis in a statute like the material witness law.

President [George W.] Bush has asserted the right—the power—to arrest any American and hold him or her indefinitely in solitary confinement, without charges, without a trial, without a lawyer. As the basis for that detention, all the president need do is designate the person an "enemy combatant." The prisoner cannot effectively challenge that designation in any court. He or she may not talk to a lawyer or family members.

Jose Padilla

That ideas may strike you as extraordinary, impossible. How could such a thing happen in the United States? But it is happening. The Bush administration has done exactly that to two Americans. I shall briefly describe what has happened to one, Jose Padilla.

Padilla was born in Brooklyn in 1971, became a gang member, served several jail sentences. He became a Muslim and travelled in, among other places, Afghanistan and Pakistan. On May 8 of last year [2002] he flew into O'Hare Airport in Chicago and was arrested by federal agents.

First Padilla was taken to New York to testify before a grand jury investigating the September 11 terrorist attack. On May 15 he was brought before a judge, who appointed a lawyer to represent him. A hearing was set for June 11. But on June 10 Attorney General Ashcroft announced that Padilla would be held as an "enemy combatant." He said Padilla was a "known terrorist" who was planning to explode a radioactive bomb. It was a conviction by announcement.

The Right to Freedom of Opinion and Expression

The Commission on Human Rights . . . calls upon States to refrain from imposing restrictions [on]:

(a) Discussion of government policies and political debate, reporting on human rights, government activities and corruption in government, engaging in peaceful demonstrations or political activities, including for peace and democracy, or expression of opinion and dissent, religion or belief;

(b) The free flow of information and ideas, including practices such as the unjustifiable banning or closing of publications or other media and the abuse of administrative measures and censorship;

(c) Access to or use of modern telecommunication technologies, including radio, television and the Internet;

(d) Journalists in situations of armed conflict.

Commission on Human Rights, 2003.

For more than 10 months now Padilla has been in a Navy brig in South Carolina. His appointed lawyer, Donna R. Newman, filed a habeas corpus action on his behalf in federal court in New York. The government, in its response, produced a declaration by a Defense Department official, Michael H. Mobbs, saying that Padilla was an enemy combatant. Government lawyers argued that that statement, without witnesses or cross-examination, was enough to justify detaining Padilla indefinitely. Courts, it said, had to defer to the president during the war on terrorism.[3] . . .

Need to Protect Constitutional Rights

What we know about Jose Padilla does not make him sound like a prince among men. But constitutional rights have to

---

3. As of this writing, Padilla was still being held in South Carolina.

be defended for the despised and the rejected if the rest of us are to be safe. Indeed, most great constitutional decisions have involved less than admirable characters. . . .

Remember also that the government, all governments, habitually exaggerate the damage that will be done to national security if courts apply the Constitution. When *The New York Times* in 1971 began publishing the Pentagon Papers, a secret history of the Vietnam War, the Nixon administration said immense harm would be done if the courts did not stop it. On the fourth day of publication, counsel for *The Times*, Alexander Bickel, said drily to the judge, "Your Honour, the Republic still stands." The Supreme Court allowed publication to go ahead, and no one has ever pointed to any resulting damage to national security.

I began by saying that lawyers and journalists have a crucial role these days in protecting our freedom. I think the distortion of the material witness statute to detain people in secret for long periods, and the indefinite detention of supposed enemy combatants without access to counsel, show that liberties we have long regarded as fundamental are under serious threat. It is quite natural for us to look to lawyers in such a situation. After all, the founders of this country put their faith in a written constitution binding rulers and the ruled alike; and that puts an inescapable obligation on lawyers and judges. . . .

Importance of an Enlightened Press

There is an obligation on the press, too, to be on guard when an administration claims that national security requires repression of civil liberties. Justice Potter Stewart of the Supreme Court explained why in his opinion in the Pentagon Papers case. On national security matters, he said, Congress and the courts are often reluctant to exercise their constitutional check on the executive. And so:

> The only effective restraint upon executive policy and power . . . may lie in an enlightened citizenry—in an informed and critical public opinion which alone can protect the values of democratic government. For this reason, it is perhaps here that a press that is alert, aware and free most vitally serves the basic purpose of the First Amendment. For without an informed and free press there cannot be an enlightened citizenry.

To Justice Stewart's adjectives for the kind of press needed to check executive claims of power in the national security area—"alert," "aware," "informed"—we must add: courageous. It may not be comfortable to take a hard look at what the Bush administration is doing under the claim of necessity in the war on terror. Reporters and editors and broadcasters are likely to find themselves denounced as unpatriotic if they are too probing, too skeptical. Attorney General Aschroft explicitly charged his critics with aiding the enemy. In Senate testimony he said:

> To those who scare peace-loving people with phantoms, of lost liberty, my message is this: Your tactics only aid terrorists, for they erode our national unity and diminish our resolve. They give ammunition to America's enemies.

Government Has Threatened Our Constitutional Values

Newspapers have had episodic stories about Jose Padilla . . . and a few stories about those detained as material witnesses. But I do not feel in the coverage any real sense of what is at stake for all of us. That is the rule of law.

When I first heard about the Bush administration's claim of power to hold people in prison forever without access to a lawyer, I expected to see major press coverage. I have not seen that. The subject has not made the front page. There has been no print and certainly no broadcast treatment equal to the government's profound challenge to our constitutional values.

The press has also given at best episodic coverage to other repressive measures by the administration since 9/11 [the September 11, 2001, terrorist attacks]. Aliens in this country as visitors, students and even permanent residents have been subjected to some harsh treatment. More than 1,100 were detained in secret and held for as much as six months while they were investigated. Many were then charged with minor visa violations such as not taking enough courses. We do not know the exact number treated that way because the Justice Department, after announcing the figure held for some weeks, kept it secret: another example of this government's pervasive desire for secrecy.

I have been using the word "press" to include both print and broadcast media. But special mention must be made of the craven performance of broadcasters. A month after 9/11, five major networks broadcast a taped message from [terrorist leader] Osama bin Laden. Condoleezza Rice, President Bush's national security adviser, then got top network executives on the line in a conference phone call. She asked them not to broadcast "inflammatory language" by bin Laden and warned that his tapes might include coded instructions.

The network executives agreed among themselves to broadcast only short segments of any future bin Laden tapes and avoid repeating them. Walter Isaacson of CNN said, "We're not going to step on the landmines Dr. Rice was talking about." A more candid explanation would have been, "We're afraid of looking unpatriotic." Condoleezza Rice's argument that the tapes containing coded instructions was singularly unpersuasive, since they had already been broadcast by Al Jazeera, the Arabic-language television network. As an example of an independent, courageous press, the network's performance was pathetic. . . .

Much at Stake

It takes unusual independence, and courage, to report what may deeply offend your sources. The press found those attributes in Vietnam. While the government in Washington was talking about light at the end of the tunnel, reporters on the ground in Vietnam told us about the dark reality. When the Pentagon Papers case tested the limits on what the press could say about how we got into the war, Justice Hugo L. Black wrote:

> Paramount among the responsibilities of a free press is the duty to prevent any part of the government from deceiving the people and sending them off to distant lands to die of foreign fevers and foreign shot and shell. In my view, far from deserving condemnation for their courageous reporting, *The New York Times*, *The Washington Post* and other newspapers should be commended for serving the purpose that the Founding Fathers saw so clearly. In revealing the workings of government that led to the Vietnam War, the newspapers nobly did that which the founders hoped and trusted they would do.

Perhaps something like the Vietnam War, with its mounting casualties and mounting evidence of official deception, brings out the best in us as journalists. Right now we have a task that is less dramatic, less obvious, but just as important: to guard our freedom during a war against terrorism that may last the rest of our lives.

The stakes are high. America's great strength has been produced by an open society, where every policy was subject to debate. American power in the world has been as much the power of its ideals—of freedom—as of its weapons. If terrorism leads us to close down the society, then the terrorists will have won. . . .

Speaking shortly after September 11, 2001, President Bush told Congress: "Freedom and fear are at war." In a sense different from what he meant, so they are.

"The national do-not-call registry offers consumers a tool with which they can protect their homes against intrusions that Congress has determined to be particularly invasive."

Telemarketers Should Be Censored

David Ebel

In 2003 the U.S. Federal Trade Commission created the National Do Not Call Registry where consumers can register to stop receiving calls from commercial telemarketers. Opponents of the registry have charged that it violates the First Amendment right to free speech. However, in a February 17, 2004, ruling, the U.S. Court of Appeals Tenth Circuit upheld the constitutionality of the registry. The following viewpoint is excerpted from the court's decision. Judge David Ebel explains that the list is an important protection of consumer privacy and also protects consumers from deceptive and abusive telemarketing. The registry merely gives the public the right to refuse unwanted calls, argues Ebel, and thus it cannot be seen as overregulation of speech. Ebel was appointed to the court in 1998.

As you read, consider the following questions:
1. As cited by the author, how is the National Do Not Call Registry similar to a consumer's right to avoid door-to-door peddlers?
2. Why are charitable and political callers less likely to engage in deceptive and abusive practices, according to Ebel?

David Ebel, decision, *Mainstream Marketing Services, Inc., et al. v. Federal Trade Commission et al.*, U.S. Court of Appeals Tenth Circuit, February 17, 2004.

We hold that the do-not-call registry is a valid commercial speech regulation because it directly advances the government's important interests in safeguarding personal privacy and reducing the danger of telemarketing abuse without burdening an excessive amount of speech. In other words, there is a reasonable fit between do-not-call regulations and the government's reasons for enacting them.

The Registry Is Consistent with the First Amendment

Four key aspects of the do-not-call registry convince us that it is consistent with First Amendment requirements. First, the list restricts only core commercial speech, i.e., commercial sales calls. Second, the do-not-call registry targets speech that invades the privacy of the home, a personal sanctuary that enjoys a unique status in our constitutional jurisprudence. Third, the do-not-call registry is an opt-in program that puts the choice of whether or not to restrict commercial calls entirely in the hands of consumers. Fourth, the do-not-call registry materially furthers the government's interests in combating the danger of abusive telemarketing and preventing the invasion of consumer privacy, blocking a significant number of the calls that cause these problems. Under these circumstances, we conclude that the requirements of the First Amendment are satisfied.

A number of additional features of the national do-not-call registry, although not dispositive, further demonstrate that the list is consistent with the First Amendment rights of commercial speakers. The challenged regulations do not hinder any business' ability to contact consumers by other means, such as through direct mailings or other forms of advertising. Moreover, they give consumers a number of different options to avoid calls they do not want to receive. Namely, consumers who wish to restrict some but not all commercial sales calls can do so by using company-specific do-not-call lists or by granting some businesses express permission to call. In addition, the government chose to offer consumers broader options to restrict commercial sales calls than charitable and political calls after finding that commercial calls were more intrusive and posed a greater danger of consumer abuse. The government also had evidence that the less restrictive company-specific do-not-call list did not solve the problems caused by commercial telemarketing, but it had no comparable evidence with respect to charitable and political fundraising.

An Expensive Problem

The fundamental problem with telemarketing—apart from its sheer obnoxiousness—is that it's cheap for the callers but not for those flabbergasted on the other end of the line. Constant harassment has persuaded many people to pay monthly fees for services to hamper it.

John J. Miller, *New York Times*, May 18, 2002.

The national do-not-call registry offers consumers a tool with which they can protect their homes against intrusions that Congress has determined to be particularly invasive. Just as a consumer can avoid door-to-door peddlers by placing a "No Solicitation" sign in his or her front yard, the do-not-call registry lets consumers avoid unwanted sales pitches that invade the home via telephone, if they choose to do so. We are convinced that the First Amendment does not prevent the government from giving consumers this option. . . .

Residential Privacy

In *Rowan v. United States Post Office Dep't*, the Supreme Court upheld the right of a homeowner to restrict material that could be mailed to his or her house. The Court emphasized the importance of individual privacy, particularly in the context of the home, stating that "the ancient concept that 'a man's home is his castle' into which 'not even the king may enter' has lost none of its vitality." In *Frisby v. Schultz*, the Court again stressed the unique nature of the home and recognized that "the State's interest in protecting the well-being, tranquility, and privacy of the home is certainly of the highest order in a free and civilized society.". . . As the Court held in Frisby: One important aspect of residential privacy is protection of the unwilling listener. . . . [A] special benefit of the privacy all citizens enjoy within their own walls, which the State may legislate to protect, is an ability to avoid intrusions.

Thus, we have repeatedly held that individuals are not required to welcome unwanted speech into their own homes and that the government may protect this freedom. Likewise, in *Hill v. Colorado*, the Court called the unwilling listener's interest in avoiding unwanted communication part of the broader right to be let alone that Justice [Louis] Brandeis described as "the right most valued by civilized men.". . .

Protecting Consumers from Deception and Abuse

The telemarketers assert that the do-not-call registry is unconstitutionally underinclusive because it does not apply to charitable and political callers. . . .

The national do-not-call registry is designed to reduce intrusions into personal privacy and the risk of telemarketing fraud and abuse that accompany unwanted telephone solicitation. The registry directly advances those goals. . . .

The FTC [Federal Trade Commission] has found that commercial callers are more likely than non-commercial callers to engage in deceptive and abusive practices. . . . Specifically, the FTC concluded that in charitable and political calls, a significant purpose of the call is to sell a cause, not merely to receive a donation, and that non-commercial callers thus have stronger incentives not to alienate the people they call or to engage in abusive and deceptive practices. ("Because charitable solicitation does more than inform private economic decisions and is not primarily concerned with providing information about the characteristics and costs of goods and services, it is not dealt with as a variety of purely commercial speech.") The speech regulated by the do-not-call list is therefore the speech most likely to cause the problems the government sought to alleviate in enacting that list, further demonstrating that the regulation directly advances the government's interests.

In sum, the do-not-call list directly advances the government's interests reducing intrusions upon consumer privacy and the risk of fraud or abuse by restricting a substantial number (and also a substantial percentage) of the calls that cause these problems. . . .

We hold that the national do-not-call registry is narrowly tailored because it does not over-regulate protected speech;

rather, it restricts only calls that are targeted at unwilling recipients. . . . The do-not-call registry prohibits only telemarketing calls aimed at consumers who have affirmatively indicated that they do not want to receive such calls and for whom such calls would constitute an invasion of privacy. . . .

The national do-not-call registry does not itself prohibit any speech. Instead, it merely "permits a citizen to erect a wall . . . that no advertiser may penetrate without his acquiescence." Almost by definition, the do-not-call regulations only block calls that would constitute unwanted intrusions into the privacy of consumers who have signed up for the list. Moreover, it allows consumers who feel susceptible to telephone fraud or abuse to ensure that most commercial callers will not have an opportunity to victimize them. . . .

Least-Restrictive Alternative

The telemarketers argue that it would have been less restrictive to let consumers rely on technological alternatives such as caller ID, call rejection services, and electronic devices designed to block unwanted calls. Each of these alternatives puts the cost of avoiding unwanted telemarketing calls on consumers. Furthermore, as the FCC found, "[a]lthough technology has improved to assist consumers in blocking unwanted calls, it has also evolved in such a way as to assist telemarketers in making greater numbers of calls and even circumventing such blocking technologies." Forcing consumers to compete in a technological arms race with the telemarketing industry is not an equally effective alternative to the do-not-call registry.

In sum, the do-not-call registry is narrowly tailored to restrict only speech that contributes to the problems the government seeks to redress, namely the intrusion into personal privacy and the risk of fraud and abuse caused by telephone calls that consumers do not welcome into their homes. No calls are restricted unless the recipient has affirmatively declared that he or she does not wish to receive them. Moreover, telemarketers still have the ability to contact consumers in other ways, and consumers have a number of different options in determining what telemarketing calls they will receive. Finally, there are not numerous and obvious less-burdensome alternatives that would restrict less speech while accomplishing the government's objectives equally as well. . . .

For the reasons discussed above, the government has asserted substantial interests to be served by the do-not-call registry (privacy and consumer protection), the do-not-call registry will directly advance those interests by banning a substantial amount of unwanted telemarketing calls, and the regulation is narrowly tailored because its opt-in feature ensures that it does not restrict any speech directed at a willing listener. In other words, the do-not-call registry bears a reasonable fit with the purposes the government sought to advance. Therefore, it is consistent with the limits the First Amendment imposes on laws restricting commercial speech.

"*The First Amendment principles . . . that forbid discriminating against commercial speech . . . are well-entrenched and laudable components of our current constitutional jurisprudence.*"

Censorship of Telemarketers Violates the First Amendment

Rodney Smolla

While the right to privacy in one's home has always been given strong constitutional protection in the United States, that right must be balanced with the protection of commercial speech, argues Rodney Smolla in the following viewpoint. Smolla contends that the National Do Not Call Registry, created by the Federal Trade Commission in 2003, violates the First Amendment protection of free speech. He believes that the registry, where consumers can register to stop receiving calls from commercial telemarketers, unconstitutionally discriminates between commercial speech and other types of speech, such as political or charitable. Smolla is dean and Allen Professor of Law at the School of Law, University of Richmond, Virginia.

As you read, consider the following questions:
1. Why does Smolla argue that it is becoming increasingly difficult for Americans to protect their privacy?
2. What was the Supreme Court's ruling on content-based discrimination in *Cincinnati v. Discovery Network*, as cited by the author?
3. Why might an "all or nothing" form of regulation actually burden more speech, according to Smolla?

Rodney Smolla, testimony before the U.S. Senate Committee on Commerce, Science, and Transportation, Washington, DC, September 30, 2003.

The do-not-call registry poses a conflict between two sacred American values, both of constitutional dimension, the right of privacy and freedom of speech. Privacy may be the most important emerging right of this new century. As technologies make it increasingly difficult for Americans to maintain their privacy, evolution in administrative, statutory, and constitutional law is necessary to keep pace, preserving privacy as an essential element of human dignity. Just as we make adjustments for inflation in cost-of-living indexes, we may need to think of "escalation clauses" in our legal protection for privacy. As the power to impinge on privacy increases, legal principles must escalate to meet the challenge, preserving the power of the average person to fight back against unwelcome intrusions. See, e.g., *Katz v. United States* (1967) (holding that the Fourth Amendment's guarantee against unreasonable searches extended to cover electronic eavesdropping, even though the framers of the Constitution could not have contemplated such an electronic search, because the Fourth Amendment was intended to protect "people, not places").

The Home as a "Castle"

The privacy of the home has always been at the core of English and American conceptions of privacy. The sacredness of the home as a "castle," fortress of privacy surrounded with moats of constitutional and common-law protection, is legendary and centuries old. . . . [Former British prime minister] William Pitt, in a speech before Parliament, declared the home a sanctuary against the force of government, demarking the line at which the brute power of the state must yield to the principle of privacy: "The poorest man may, in his cottage, bid defiance to all the forces of the crown. It may be frail; its roof may shake; the wind may blow through it; the storm may enter; the rain may enter; but the king of England may not enter; all his force dares not cross the threshold of the ruined tenement.". . .

This tradition was the backdrop of the Fourth Amendment, and its guarantee of the right of the people to be secure in their "persons, houses, papers, and effects" against unreasonable searches and seizures. . . .

This solicitude for the home, originally conceptualized as a bulwark against the force of the state, has evolved into a broader concept, in which the home is seen as an essential to one's autonomy and privacy, a place of respite from the cruel world. In the words of Judge Jerome Frank: "A man can still control a small part of his environment, his house; he can retreat thence from outsiders, secure in the knowledge that they cannot get at him without disobeying the Constitution. That is still a sizable hunk of liberty—worth protecting from encroachment. A sane, decent, civilized society must provide some such oasis, some shelter from public scrutiny, some insulated enclosure, some enclave, some inviolate place which is a man's castle."

Virtually everyone engaged in the debate over the do-not-call registry will concede that powerful privacy interests are at stake. Uninvited telephone solicitations are highly intrusive, particularly when they come during family time such as dinner and early evenings in the home. . . .

Protection of Commercial Speech

The vital privacy interests that animate the do-not-call registry must be balanced against the competing First Amendment protection for freedom of speech, a protection that often is dependent upon the ability of the speaker to initiate the message, making a preliminary attempt to engage the listener or reader even though the message may not have been invited.

Commercial telemarketing is a form of "commercial speech.". . .

The arc of modern commercial speech jurisprudence is unmistakable: in decision after decision the Supreme Court has advanced protection for advertising, repeatedly striking down regulations grounded in paternalistic motivations. . . .

Antipathy for Content-Based Discrimination

This antipathy [of the Supreme Court] toward content-based discrimination applies to commercial speech regulation. In a key precedent, *Cincinnati v. Discovery Network, Inc.*, the Supreme Court struck down an ordinance that engaged in content-based distinctions similar to those in the do-not-call registry. In *Discovery Network* the city of Cincinnati enacted an ordinance prohibiting the distribution of commercial handbills on public property. The ordinance effectively granted distributors of traditional "newspapers," such as the *Cincinnati Post, USA Today,* or *The Wall Street Journal,* access to public sidewalks through newsracks, while denying equivalent newsrack access to the distributors of commercial magazines and handbills, such as publications for apartment or house rentals or sales. The ordinance was designed to reduce the visual and special clutter of newsracks. The constitutional difficulty, however, was that no principled distinction could be drawn between the clutter caused by a *USA Today* newsrack and one caused by a real estate magazine. Clutter was clutter, and a newsrack was a newsrack, and the content of the speech inside the rack bore no relation to the city's environmental or aesthetic interests. The Supreme Court pointedly rejected the notion that government could simply "pick on" commercial speech, making such speech bear a disproportionate burden. . . .

Turn the Ringer Off

Your ownership of the television doesn't give you the right to prevent advertisers from broadcasting into your living room. Similarly, your ownership of a phone doesn't mean you can suppress usage of incoming lines. If you would rather eat dinner uninterrupted, just turn off the ringer. You can even use caller ID or record your messages and return them selectively.

Robert A. Levy, *National Review Online*, October 2, 2003.

The District Court in Mainstream Marketing applied similar logic. An unwanted telephone call during dinner is an unwanted telephone call during dinner. An abusive or overbearing or fraudulent call is an abusive or overbearing or fraudulent call. Whether the caller is a commercial vendor, a solicitor for a charity, or a political fundraiser, the essential hit on privacy interests remains the same. Similarly, the District Court could find nothing in the record before it to support the supposition that commercial telemarketers are as a class more prone to abuse or fraudulent practices than non-commercial telemarketers. . . .

Regulation Must Be "All or Nothing"

The First Amendment principles forbidding content-discrimination, and the specific commercial speech principles that forbid discriminating against commercial speech on grounds that are unrelated to the commercial content of the speech, are well-entrenched and laudable components of our current constitutional jurisprudence. There are sound reasons why courts look with great skepticism at content-based distinctions, and sound reasons why these principles apply to advertising and commercial speech. There is probably no principle more central to our First Amendment tradition than the notion that the government ought not "pick and choose" among messages, particularly when the values it seeks to vindicate bear no demonstrable relationship to the content of those messages.

In short, modern First Amendment doctrine tends to favor an "all or nothing" form of regulation. There is, admittedly, an irony here, and a heavy social cost. To eliminate the distinction between non-commercial and commercial telemarketing would actually burden more speech. One might plausibly argue that the current form of the do-not-call registry is thus actually preferable to a complete ban. Reinforcing this argument, one might argue that given the especially high place that charitable and political speech enjoy in our constitutional constellation, there is positive constitutional value in carving out an exception for those categories. Seen this way, the current do-not-call registry regime does not discriminate against commercial speech so much as it discriminates in favor of political or charitable solicitations. While these arguments do have some appeal, in the end they appear to be in tension with current First Amendment doctrines.

Periodical Bibliography

The following articles have been selected to supplement the diverse views presented in this chapter.

Doug Bandow — "Free to Be Stupid," *Ideas on Liberty*, March 2002.

Stephen Chapman — "When Censorship Isn't Censorship," *Conservative Chronicle*, August 28, 2002.

Charles Haynes — "T-Shirt Rebellion in the Land of the Free," www.firstamendmentcenter.org, March 14, 2004.

Daniel Henninger — "How Our Age Dumbed Down Even Invective," *Wall Street Journal*, May 17, 2002.

Nat Hentoff — "Racism and Free Speech," *Village Voice*, February 22, 2000.

John Leo — "Campus Censors in Retreat," *U.S. News & World Report*, February 16, 2004.

Adam Liptak — "Symbols and Free Speech," *New York Times*, December 15, 2002.

Kenan Malik — "Protect the Freedom to Shock," *New Statesman*, August 13, 2001.

Mark O'Keefe — "Foul Words Permeate Pop Culture, Eliciting a Backlash," *Christian Century*, April 6, 2004.

Leonard Pitts — "First Amendment? What About Simple Respect?" *Los Angeles Business Journal*, May 13, 2002.

Will Potter — "Sense and Censorship," *Chronicle of Higher Education*, November 14, 2003.

Rhoda Rabkin — "Do Kids Need Government Censors?" *Policy Review*, February 2002.

Bruce Shapiro — "Censorship 101," *Nation*, December 23, 2002.

Stuart Taylor Jr. — "How Campus Censors Squelch Freedom of Speech," *National Journal*, July 12, 2003.

CHAPTER 2

Should the Internet Be Censored?

Chapter Preface

In 1999 nineteen-year-old Shawn Fanning created an online file-sharing service called Napster. This service allowed its users to easily share music files with people all around the world. Using Napster, anyone with a computer and an Internet connection could download, free of charge, any file they wanted from another user. Over the next two years, millions of people used Napster to download music, movies, computer software, and other types of files. Unfortunately, many of the files being downloaded by these users were protected by copyright law, which states that the creator of a work has the exclusive right to reproduce, distribute, and publicly perform that work. By downloading music without first receiving permission, Napster users were violating copyright law. In late 1999 several major recording companies filed a lawsuit against Napster for copyright infringement, and in 2001, file sharing on Napster was shut down.

File sharing is just one example of how online communication has proliferated, enabling people to easily and anonymously share ideas and information online. However, as the Napster case illustrates, this increased ease of expression on the Internet has also led to an increased risk of violating the rights of others, leading many observers to call for Internet censorship.

Many people believe that the nature of the Internet makes it impossible to censor content in order to prevent copyright violations. When Napster's free file-sharing service was halted, dozens of similar sites immediately sprang up to take its place. While the music industry has brought numerous lawsuits against individuals engaged in illegal sharing of copyrighted music, the practice continues to be widespread. According to writer Ray Gerard, the anonymity and the international nature of the Internet make it impossible to effectively protect copyrights. He observes: "It has become nearly impossible to monitor the actions of any one person on this world wide inter-network. The non-centralized nature of the Internet makes it very difficult for any company, organization, or government to observe or control what types of data are transferred from user to user."

However, others point out that copyright law is enforced in all other arenas of society and they believe that the Internet should be no different. They contend that some Internet regulation can, and should, be enforced. The National Music Publishers' Association's Internet Anti-Piracy Task Force is one advocate of Internet regulation. It argues that copyrights must be strictly enforced on the Internet in order to protect the creators of original works and ideas. According to the task force,

> Violating the copyright laws by posting, downloading or sending protected works over the Internet or other computer networks without authorization of the copyright owner, is unfair, unlawful, and ultimately counter to the interest of honest Internet citizens. . . . At no time in history has it been more important for the public to recognize the value of copyright protection than in the Information Age. . . . Since the power of the Internet can, with the mere push of a button, easily destroy the global monetary value of a work to its author, copyright protections may be even more important in the virtual world than in the physical one.

Copyright protection is only one of many controversial debates that have been spurred by the Internet. Critics on both sides continue to argue fiercely about how much free expression should be allowed on the Internet, and whether it needs to be balanced with some type of regulation. In the following chapter various authors discuss whether it is possible, or desirable, to censor the Internet.

"Because of the vast quantity of material on the Internet, . . . libraries cannot possibly segregate . . . all the Internet material that is appropriate for inclusion from all that is not."

Internet Filters Should Be Used in Libraries

William H. Rehnquist

In June 2003 the U.S. Supreme Court ruled that libraries should be required to install Internet filters on their computers in order to receive federal funding. In the following viewpoint, excerpted from the Court's ruling, Chief Justice William H. Rehnquist argues that filters are the most effective way to block access to pornographic sites and that their use is consistent with the public library goal of collecting material that will have the greatest benefit to the community. While filters may occasionally block medical and other nonpornographic sites, states Rehnquist, they provide necessary protection for children, and adult library patrons can easily request that the filter be disabled or a site unblocked. Rehnquist was sworn in to the Supreme Court in 1972 and became chief justice in 1986.

As you read, consider the following questions:
1. A filter set to block pornography may also block sites that are neither obscene nor pornographic. How can the library minimize this problem, according to Rehnquist?
2. What are the missions of public libraries, as cited by the author?

William H. Rehnquist, majority opinion, *United States et al. v. American Library Association, Inc., et al.*, Washington, DC, U.S. Supreme Court, June 23, 2003.

B y connecting to the Internet, public libraries provide patrons with a vast amount of valuable information. But there is also an enormous amount of pornography on the Internet, much of which is easily obtained. The accessibility of this material has created serious problems for libraries, which have found that patrons of all ages, including minors, regularly search for online pornography. Some patrons also expose others to pornographic images by leaving them displayed on Internet terminals or printed at library printers.

Upon discovering these problems, Congress became concerned that the E-rate and LSTA [Library Services and Technology Act] programs [which provide federal funding for library Internet use] were facilitating access to illegal and harmful pornography. Congress learned that adults "use library computers to access pornography that is then exposed to staff, passersby, and children," and that "minors access child and adult pornography in libraries."

Filtering Is an Effective Solution

But Congress also learned that filtering software that blocks access to pornographic Web sites could provide a reasonably effective way to prevent such uses of library resources. . . . A library can set such software to block categories of material, such as "Pornography" or "Violence." When a patron tries to view a site that falls within such a category, a screen appears indicating that the site is blocked. But a filter set to block pornography may sometimes block other sites that present neither obscene nor pornographic material, but that nevertheless trigger the filter. To minimize this problem, a library can set its software to prevent the blocking of material that falls into categories like "Education," "History," and "Medical." A library may also add or delete specific sites from a blocking category, and anyone can ask companies that furnish filtering software to unblock particular sites.

Responding to this information, Congress enacted CIPA [Children's Internet Protection Act]. It provides that a library may not receive E-rate or LSTA assistance unless it has "a policy of Internet safety for minors that includes the operation of a technology protection measure . . . that protects against access" by any persons to "visual depictions" that constitute "obscen[ity]" or "child pornography," and that protects against access by minors to "visual depictions" that are "harmful to minors."...

Libraries Select Materials to Benefit the Community

Public libraries pursue the worthy missions of facilitating learning and cultural enrichment. . . . ALA's [American Library Association] Library Bill of Rights states that libraries should provide "books and other . . . resources . . . for the interest, information, and enlightenment of all people of the community the library serves." To fulfill their traditional missions, public libraries must have broad discretion to decide what material to provide to their patrons. Although they seek to provide a wide array of information, their goal has never been to provide "universal coverage." Instead, public libraries seek to provide materials "that would be of the greatest direct benefit or interest to the community." To this end, libraries collect only those materials deemed to have "requisite and appropriate quality."...

A library's need to exercise judgment in making collection decisions depends on its traditional role in identifying suit-

Asay. © by Charles Asay. Reproduced by permission.

able and worthwhile material; it is no less entitled to play that role when it collects material from the Internet than when it collects material from any other source. Most libraries already exclude pornography from their print collections because they deem it inappropriate for inclusion. We do not subject these decisions to heightened scrutiny; it would make little sense to treat libraries' judgments to block online pornography any differently, when these judgments are made for just the same reason.

Filters Are Consistent with Library Goals

Moreover, because of the vast quantity of material on the Internet and the rapid pace at which it changes, libraries cannot possibly segregate, item by item, all the Internet material that is appropriate for inclusion from all that is not. While a library could limit its Internet collection to just those sites it found worthwhile, it could do so only at the cost of excluding an enormous amount of valuable information that it lacks the capacity to review. Given that tradeoff, it is entirely reasonable for public libraries to reject that approach and instead exclude certain categories of content, without making individualized judgments that everything they do make available has requisite and appropriate quality. . . .

Filters Can Be Disabled for Adults

[There is a] tendency of filtering software to "overblock"— that is, to erroneously block access to constitutionally protected speech that falls outside the categories that software users intend to block. . . . Assuming that such erroneous blocking presents constitutional difficulties, any such concerns are dispelled by the ease with which patrons may have the filtering software disabled. When a patron encounters a blocked site, he need only ask a librarian to unblock it or (at least in the case of adults) disable the filter. . . . Libraries have the capacity to permanently unblock any erroneously blocked site. . . . [Some people view] unblocking and disabling as inadequate because some patrons may be too embarrassed to request them. But the Constitution does not guarantee the right to acquire information at a public library without any risk of embarrassment.

"If you're an adult, I would rather let you decide what sites you want to see, not the government or its mandated computer filters."

Internet Filters Should Not Be Used in Libraries

Clarence Page

The U.S. Supreme Court, in June 2003, ruled that libraries should be required to install Internet filters on their computers in order to receive federal funding. Libraries should not be required to install Internet filters on their computers, argues Clarence Page in the following viewpoint. While these filters are designed to block only pornography, they actually block a large quantity of nonpornographic material as well, he maintains. Instead of mandating filters, Page believes the government should let librarians take responsibility for protecting children from pornographic materials on library computers. Page is a columnist and member of the editorial staff of the *Chicago Tribune*. In 1987 he was awarded the American Civil Liberties Union James P. McGuire Award for his columns on constitutional rights.

As you read, consider the following questions:

1. What type of important Web sites might filtering programs block, according to the author?
2. Which ethnic groups are more likely to depend on library Internet access and thus be more likely to have that access censored by library filters, according to Page?
3. According to the author, why might it be difficult to disable filters at the requests of individual library users?

Clarence Page, "When Smut Filters Block Too Much," *The Chicago Tribune*, June 29, 2003, p. 11. Copyright © 2003 by *The Chicago Tribune*. Reproduced by permission.

If you are reading this column online, you may have an unfiltered computer to thank or, depending on your point of view, to curse.

The last time I criticized federal efforts to block pornography and other foul things that children should not see on the Internet, I received an unwelcome taste of government censorship.

A sympathetic reader informed me that, as an experiment, he tried to call up the column on a filtered computer.

Sure enough, the filter blocked access to it.

The government censors, in this case, were anti-smut filters like those that the Children's Internet Protection Act [CIPA] orders all libraries to install on their computers to receive federal funding.

Blocking Non-Pornographic Information

After Congress passed CIPA in 2000, court challenges held it in abeyance until the Supreme Court last week [in July 2003] decided to ignore my advice and uphold it.

Filtering programs offer a poor remedy for Web porn, I wrote. Either they don't work well enough to block all access to objectionable material or they work so well that a word like "breast," for example, can block your access to important information about breast cancer.

Well, my examples of trigger words probably triggered anti-porn filters. I got blocked. Muzzled. Censored.

Yes, fellow Americans, it happened right here in the good old U.S. of A.

Of course, filtering errors vary with the program and with its settings. A study by the Kaiser Family Foundation late last year [2002] found the six most commonly used filters incorrectly blocked just 1.4 percent of health sites at their weakest setting and 24 percent at their highest.

Health sites that mentioned "condoms" or "safe sex" were blocked most often, from 9 percent at the weakest setting to 50 percent at the strongest.

Meanwhile, the amount of blocked porn increased only marginally, from 87 percent at the weakest level to 91 percent at the strongest.

Either way, if you're an adult, I would rather let you decide what sites you want to see, not the government or its mandated computer filters.

So would most librarians, according to the American Library Association [ALA], which opposed the filtering law. About half of the nation's libraries use some filters, although often only in the children's sections, estimates Judith Krug, director of the ALA's Office of Intellectual Freedom. Somehow those libraries have managed the computer porn problem just fine without Congress' help during the 2½ years that CIPA has been waiting to go into effect. No more.

CIPA Is a Violation of Free Speech Rights

Rather than allowing local decision makers to tailor their responses to local problems, the Children's Internet Protection Act (CIPA) operates as a blunt nationwide restraint on adult access to "an enormous amount of valuable information" that individual librarians cannot possibly review. Most of that information is constitutionally protected speech. In my view, this restraint in unconstitutional.

Until a blocked site or group of sites is unblocked, a patron is unlikely to know what is being hidden and therefore whether there is any point in asking for the filter to be removed. It is as though the statute required a significant part of every library's reading materials to be kept in unmarked, locked rooms or cabinets, which could be opened only in response to specific requests. Some curious readers would in time obtain access to the hidden materials, but many would not. Inevitably, the interest of the authors of those works in reaching the widest possible audience would be abridged. Moreover, because the procedures that different libraries are likely to adopt to respond to unblocking requests will no doubt vary, it is impossible to measure the aggregate effect of the statute on patrons' access to blocked sites. Unless we assume that the statute is a mere symbolic gesture, we must conclude that it will create a significant prior restraint on adult access to protected speech.

—*Justice Stevens*

David L. Sobel, www.firstamendment.org, October 2003.

Ironically, the belated CIPA widens the digital divide that federal funds were intended to close. CIPA will impose its burden mainly on those who depend on libraries for their computer access.

Ten percent of Internet users get access through a library, according to the Commerce Department. Blacks and Hispanics are more likely than whites or Asians to be in that group. Users tend to be poor and non-white. They also tend to use libraries that can least afford to reject federal funding in order to keep unfiltered access.

CIPA Should Be Repealed

The high court's decision written by Chief Justice William Rehnquist agrees with the Bush administration that this is not a problem. Users can simply request that librarians disable the filters, he wrote. But that's not easy, librarians say, since filters tend to be installed system-wide, not switched on and off at the individual computer-unit.

Justice Anthony Kennedy in a separate opinion suggested a new option for the law's opponents to take. If the filtering industry fails to come up with easier and better filters, the law's opponents might be able to file a new challenge.

The ALA officials I interviewed last week [in July 2003] bristled at that suggestion. They agreed with the goal, but the tactic might put their organization in the awkward position of backing a suit against one of their member libraries.

Of course, there's another possibility. Impatient citizens might tell their senators and congressmen to repeal CIPA and let librarians and local community do what they do best, which is to manage their libraries.

You might want to express your feelings in an e-mail to Capitol Hill. But please watch your language. You don't want to get blocked.

"Our Constitution protects speech, it does not protect obscenity. The President and the Justice Department . . . must . . . pursue violations of the laws [that restrict obscenity]."

Internet Pornography Should Be Censored

J. Robert Flores

Internet pornography is a threat to American society and should be censored, argues J. Robert Flores in the following viewpoint, which was originally given as congressional testimony on May 23, 2000. According to Flores, the U.S. government has the power to effectively prosecute pornographers and could thus lead the rest of the world in reducing obscene material on the Internet. Flores is administrator for the Office of Juvenile Justice and Delinquency Prevention, an organization that works to prevent juvenile delinquency and victimization.

As you read, consider the following questions:
1. How do pornographers push their products on the Internet, as cited by Flores?
2. Where does most Internet obscenity originate from, according to the author?
3. Why does Flores believe a comprehensive and coherent strategy to reduce obscenity is necessary?

J. Robert Flores, address before the Subcommittee on Telecommunications, Trade, and Consumer Protection, Committee on Commerce, Washington, DC, May 23, 2000.

[S]ince 1995] much has changed in the size and nature of the Internet based pornography industry, mostly on the World Wide Web and Usenet newsgroups. In late 1995, few of the major pornographers had a major presence on the Net. While the amount of material that was then available was astounding by anyone's count, today it is available in quantities and formats that make it a ubiquitous commodity. Today, obscenity merchants have gone public, as in the NASDAQ [stock market] and other capital markets. *Forbes* [magazine] reports that [in 2000] "pornography to the tune of $1 billion already flows over the Internet."

A Threat to Society

In addition to the change in the amount of material on the Internet, a look at what now comprises a sizeable and growing portion of hard-core obscenity, should send shivers up the spine of every person of good will. Today, adult pornography sites have moved to feature, as a predominant theme, sexually explicit material which is marketed as depicting "teen", "young", "Lolita", "virgin", and "high school" girls and boys. Once the sole province of child pornographers, this jargon and code has now become a staple of adult obscenity marketers.

Does this threaten children? You better believe it does. Our kids and grand-kids see it and become indoctrinated by it. Pedophiles and porn addicts see it and become incited by it. Even the U.S. Supreme Court recognized that the mere existence of child pornography images is an ongoing danger to children, because of the stimulating effect it has on pedophiles and the seductive effect it has on children. . . .

The pornography industry has also become among the most aggressive marketers on the Internet, using newly developed "push" technologies alongside offensive and fraudulent marketing ploys. Thus, even if it were ever true, and I doubt it, that only those who sought out obscenity could find it, today only a lucky few are able to avoid it, as the Internet user community is bombarded with advertisements, tricked into visiting sites, given hot links to porn when search engines are asked for innocent sites, sent unsolicited porn spam e-mails, and trapped in endless mousetraps that bounce them from porn site to porn site when they try and leave. . . .

Pornographers Must Be Prosecuted

The frequently heard argument that we really can't do anything about Internet obscenity because so much of it comes from overseas is specious. Most of the world's hard-core obscenity comes from America's porn syndicates and they are subject to U.S. law no matter where they send their criminal materials from or to. Hiding their Web servers overseas won't save them, we can still prosecute American criminals in U.S. District Courts and seize their assets and credit card receipts from U.S. banks. . . .

Contrary to the complaints made by some, the courts have consistently made clear that federal obscenity law applies in cyberspace as it does in real life. . . .

As a practical matter, I believe that federal investigators and prosecutors can and must bring cases which would make a difference for average families and which would be a giant step towards stopping sexual exploitation. For example, prosecutions can be brought against the Web site owners who most directly profit from this form of human exploitation. The producers and distributors of movies, pictures, and other obscene material who wholesale them to the Web sites for resale can also be pursued under existing law. The recruiters and procurers of women who run virtual prostitution operations making live images available through the Internet may also be prosecuted for transmitting obscenity. And finally, those who bankroll these operations, many of whom have historically been organized criminal operations, may also be investigated and prosecuted.

The United States Should Lead the War Against Obscenity

Leaders and businesses in Europe, Asia, Latin America, and our other trading partners look to the United States to see what we, the major source of obscenity worldwide, will do with this form of exploitation. In fact, there is a 1911 Treaty on the Suppression of Obscene Publications that would provide an existing framework for international cooperation to deal with hard-core obscenity on the Internet and World Wide Web. That Treaty is still in force and now has at least 126 member countries as signatory nations, including most of the Americas, Europe, and Asia. We seek to lead in every other Internet related area, why not here as well. Can money be made by this industry? Of course. In fact, it is one of the few guaranteed ways to succeed financially on the Internet. But at what cost? It is not free, either to the people who consume the products or the society where it runs rampant. We cannot fail to lead simply on the assumption that some amount of obscenity comes from overseas. To do that would be to turn over our Country and its safety to pornographers and sex business operators who are savvy enough to move their servers and remote offices overseas. We don't do it in any other area of criminal law, why would we start here?

Our Constitution protects speech, it does not protect obscenity. The President and the Justice Department in particular must recognize that difference and fulfill their obligation to pursue violations of the laws passed by Congress. Mindlessly investigating and prosecuting cases, whether child pornography, child stalking, or even obscenity, will not make children and adults safe from being assaulted by material that is not only offensive but illegal. A comprehensive and coherent strategy which addresses each of the major aspects of the obscenity and sex business operations is necessary.

"How can the government's policy [of reducing Internet pornography] possibly achieve its stated goals, without creating an unprecedentedly intrusive censorship machinery?"

The Government Should Not Censor Internet Pornography

Eugene Volokh

There is no way for the United States to reduce Internet pornography without imposing harsh, unconstitutional censorship, argues Eugene Volokh in the following viewpoint. A comprehensive government-mandated filtering system, or the prosecution of porn users might be effective, states Volokh, however these measures threaten the First Amendment protection of free speech. Moreover, imprisoning U.S. pornographers will merely push the industry into other countries, he believes. Volokh is a professor of law at the University of California, Los Angeles, School of Law. He teaches free speech law, copyright law, and the law of government and religion.

As you read, consider the following questions:

1. According to Volokh, what is the only approach that really has any hope of reducing the accessibility of porn to Americans?
2. Why does nationwide government filtering sound like a violation of the First Amendment, as cited by the author?
3. Why does Volokh believe that other countries will be unlikely to join America's campaign against pornography?

So here's what I wonder about the Justice Department's planned new [in 2004] obscenity crackdown. As we know, there's lots of porn of all varieties out there on the Internet. I don't know how much of it is produced in the U.S.—but even if it's 75 percent, and every single U.S. producer is shut down, wouldn't foreign sites happily take up the slack?

Production Will Move Off-Shore

It's not like Americans have some great irreproducible national skills in smut-making, or like it takes a $100 million Hollywood budget to make a porn movie. Foreign porn will doubtless be quite an adequate substitute for the U.S. market. Plus the foreign distributors might even be able to make and distribute copies of the existing U.S.-produced stock—I doubt that the imprisoned copyright owners will be suing them for infringement (unless the U.S. government seizes the copyrights, becomes the world #1 pornography owner, starts trying to enforce the copyrights against overseas distributors, and gets foreign courts to honor those copyrights, which is far from certain and likely far from cheap).

And even if overall world production of porn somehow improbably falls by 75 percent, will that seriously affect the typical porn consumer's diet? Does it matter whether you have, say, 100,000 porn titles (and live feeds) to choose from, or just 25,000? So we have three possible outcomes:

(1) The U.S. spends who knows how many prosecutorial and technical resources going after U.S. pornographers. A bunch of them get imprisoned. U.S. consumers keep using the same amount of porn as before. Maybe they can't get porn on cable channels or in hotel rooms any more, but they can get more than they ever wanted on the Internet. Nor do I think that the crackdown will somehow subtly affect consumers' attitudes about the morality of porn—it seems highly unlikely that potential porn consumers will decide to stop getting it because they hear that some porn producers are being prosecuted.

The only potential benefit: If you really think that the porn industry is very bad for its actors, you're at least sparing Americans that harm, and shifting it off-shore instead. Other than that: The investment of major prosecutorial resources yields a net practical benefit of roughly zero.

(2) The government gets understandably outraged by the "foreign smut loophole." "Given all the millions that we've invested in going after the domestic porn industry, how can we tolerate all our work being undone by foreign filth-peddlers?," pornography prosecutors and their political allies would ask. So they unveil the solution, in fact pretty much the only solution that will work: Nationwide filtering.

It's true: Going after cyberporn isn't really that tough—if you require every service provider in the nation to block access to all sites that are on a constantly updated government-run "Forbidden Off-Shore Site" list. Of course, there couldn't be any trials applying community standards and the like before a site is added to the list; that would take far too long. The government would have to be able to just order a site instantly blocked, without any hearing with an opportunity for the other side to respond, since even a quick response would take up too much time, and would let the porn sites just move from location to location every several weeks.

Sure, that sounds like a violation of First Amendment procedural rules, even when the government is going after substantively unprotected obscenity. Sure, that would make it easier for the government to put all sorts of other sites on the list. Sure, it's a substantially more intrusive step than any of the Internet regulations we've seen so far, and is substantially more intrusive in some ways than virtually any speech restriction in American history. (I say in some ways, not in all ways, since it would have a limited substantive focus—but the procedure would be unprecedently restrictive, and First Amendment law has always recognized the practical importance of procedure.) But it's the only approach that has any hope of really reducing the accessibility of porn to American consumers.

(3) Finally, the government can go after the users: Set up "honeypot" sites (seriously, that would be the technically correct name for them) that would look like normal offshore pornography sites. Draw people in to buy the stuff. Figure out who the buyers are (you'd have to ban any anonymizer Web sites that might be used to hide such transactions, by setting up some sort of mandatory filtering such as what I de-

The Right of Individual Choice

The Constitution exists precisely so that opinions and judgments, including esthetic and moral judgments about art and literature, can be formed, tested, and expressed. What the Constitution says is that these judgments are for the individual to make, not for the Government to decree, even with the mandate or approval of a majority. Technology expands the capacity to choose; and it denies the potential of this revolution if we assume the Government is best positioned to make these choices for us.

Supreme Court justice Anthony M. Kennedy, *United States et al. v. Playboy Entertainment Group, Inc.*, May 22, 2000.

scribed in option (2). Then arrest them and prosecute them. Heck, lock each one up for several years like you would a child porn buyer. Make him register as a sex offender. Seize his house on the theory that it's a forfeitable asset, since it was used to facilitate an illegal transaction. All because he, or he and his wife, like to get turned on by watching pictures of people having sex. Then repeat for however many people it takes to get everyone scared of the Smut Police.

Three Undesirable Outcomes

So we really have three possible outcomes:

(1) The crackdown on porn is doomed to be utterly ineffective at preventing the supposedly harmful effects of porn on its viewers, and on the viewers' neighbors.

(2) The crackdown on porn will be made effective—by implementing a comprehensive government-mandated filtering system run by some administrative agency that constantly monitors the Net and requires private service providers to block any sites that the agency says are obscene.

(3) The crackdown on porn will turn into a full-fledged War on Smut that will be made effective by prosecuting, imprisoning, and seizing the assets of porn buyers.

Seriously, I don't see many other alternatives. The government could try to put pressure on financial intermediaries, for instance requiring Visa and MasterCard to refuse transactions with certain locations; but unless that's made just as intrusive as option #2 above, it will be hopelessly ineffective, since sites can easily just periodically change their payee names, or use various offshore intermediaries. The government might also try to persuade foreign countries to join its campaign, but I'm pretty sure that won't work, either. First, the Europeans are apparently fairly tolerant of much porn; and, second, I highly doubt that we can persuade every poor third-world country, some of which have thriving trades in real flesh, to spend its resources creating and actually enforcing anti-porn laws, in the face of whatever payoffs the porn industry is willing to provide.

So, supporters of the Justice Department's plans, which do you prefer—#1, #2, or #3? Note that I'm not asking whether porn is bad, or whether porn should be constitutionally protected. I'm certainly not asking whether we'd be better off in some hypothetical porn-free world (just like no sensible debate about alcohol, drug, or gun policy should ask whether we'd be better off in some hypothetical alcohol-, drug-, or gun-free world).

I'm asking: How can the government's policy possibly achieve its stated goals, without creating an unprecedentedly intrusive censorship machinery, one that's far, far beyond what the Justice Department is talking about right now?

"Stemming this rising tide [of spam] is essential if the Internet is to continue to be an effective medium of communication and commerce."

Regulations Should Be Implemented to Reduce Spam

Charles E. Schumer

Unsolicited commercial e-mail, or spam, is growing at an exponential rate, and threatening families, businesses, and the economy, argues Charles E. Schumer in the following viewpoint, which was originally given as testimony before the Senate on May 21, 2003. Schumer contends that large quantities of spam are threatening to cause gridlock on the Internet, and that spam costs U.S. businesses billions of dollars every year. In addition, he voices concern that many of these e-mails are harmful to consumers because they advertise pornographic Web sites or are used to perpetrate crimes such as identity theft. He maintains that it is vitally important for the government to enact regulation to limit spam. Schumer is a U.S. senator representing New York State. He serves as a member on the Judiciary Committee and the Committee on Rules and Administration.

As you read, consider the following questions:

1. What type of junk e-mail is Schumer powerless to stop his daughter from receiving?
2. What percentage of e-mail traffic qualifies as spam, according to the author?
3. How is legitimate commercial e-mail harmed by spam, according to Schumer?

Charles E. Schumer, testimony before the U.S. Senate Committee on Commerce, Science, and Transportation, Washington, DC, May 21, 2003.

I believe we are under siege. Armies of online marketers have overrun email inboxes across the country with advertisements for herbal remedies, get-rich-quick schemes and pornography.

As you are all aware, spam traffic is growing at a geometric rate, causing the Superhighway to enter a state of virtual gridlock. What was a simple annoyance last year [2002] has become a major concern this year and could cripple one of the greatest inventions of the 20th century next year if nothing is done.

Way back in 1999, the average email user received just 40 pieces of unsolicited commercial email—what we call spam—each year. This year, the number is expected to pass 2,500. I know that I'm lucky if I don't get 40 pieces of spam every couple of days!

As a result, a revolution against spam is brewing as the epidemic of junk email exacts an ever increasing toll on families, businesses and the economy.

Let me illustrate this point with a story. My wife and I have two wonderful children, one of whom is just about to complete her first year at college. The other, a 14 year-old girl, is an absolute whiz on the Internet who loves sending and receiving email.

As parents, we do our best to make sure she has good values and that the Internet is a positive experience for her—a device to help her with her schoolwork or learn about events taking place around the world and maybe even a way to order the latest *NSYNC CD.

You can imagine my anger and dismay when I discovered that not only was she a victim of spam like myself, but, like all email users, much of the junk email she was receiving advertise pornographic web sites. I was and remain virtually powerless to prevent such garbage from reaching my daughter's inbox. The frustration I feel in the battle against spam is one that I think business owners and Internet Service Providers [ISPs] across that nation can identify with.

According to Ferris Research, spam costs businesses in the United States $10 billion each year in lost productivity, consumption of Information Technology resources and help-desk time. With surveys showing that over 40% of email traffic qualities as spam, ISPs spend millions of dollars each year on research, filtering software and new servers to deal with the ever expanding volume of junk email being sent through their pipes.

And, if the spam itself isn't enough, spammers often engage in crimes such as identity theft and fraud to secure email addresses and domain names from which to send millions of pieces of junk email.

Regulation Needed

All of this demonstrates that it's time to take back the Internet from the spammers. And why I am joining you today in saying that enough is enough.

We all know that spammers use a variety of tools and methods to send millions of email messages each day. In order to be effective, I believe spam solutions will have to be as creative and varied as the spammers' efforts.

We should give law enforcement officials, ISPs and others a wide variety of tools to fight spam. Among the possible solutions that exist—and this is not an exhaustive list—are pending legislation in the Senate and the House that would enact anti-email harvesting provisions and special email labeling requirements; stipulate valid unsubscribe features; and prohibit false and fraudulent header, router and subject line information.[1]

And that's just a start. As I said before, because of the dramatic challenges we face in stemming the spam flood, we need a multi-pronged approach.

In particular, I believe stiff criminal penalties—including jail time for repeat offenders—are warranted. I am working with my colleagues in the Judiciary Committee on a bill to create these new penalties.

We will hunt down spammers one by one, using criminal penalties to show what will happen to those who continue to send junk email.

Another idea I have offered is a National No-Spam Reg-

1. In December 2003 the CAN-SPAM Act was signed into law. It establishes the first national standards for the sending of commercial email with penalties for the violation of these rules.

Spam Is a Large and Growing Problem

April 2001	683,579
May 2001	930,546
June 2001	879,253
July 2001	1,018,737
August 2001	1,504,043
September 2001	1,457,337
October 2001	1,692,333
November 2001	1,956,529
December 2001	1,969,041
January 2002	2,777,017
February 2002	3,187,430
March 2002	3,773,738
April 2002	4,339,799
May 2002	4,686,983
June 2002	4,825,144
July 2002	4,971,097
August 2002	5,065,858
September 2002	5,285,404
October 2002	5,352,325
November 2002	5,503,246
December 2002	5,915,062
January 2003	6,092,514
February 2003	6,458,065
March 2003	6,716,387
April 2003	7,018,625

Enrique Salem, congressional testimony, May 21, 2003. Information obtained by Brightman's Probe Network.

istry. This list, maintained by the Federal Trade Commission, would be a gigantic database of people who have "opted out" of receiving spam by submitting their email addresses to the list.

The list is modeled on the highly successful Do-Not-Call registries that have been used to ward off telemarketers.

Although a similar list for email addresses poses security challenges that must be addressed before implementation, I am hopeful that this list might be one way we can give consumers control over their in-boxes.

Protecting Legitimate Commerce

None of these solutions will be the silver bullet that stops all spam. But a multi-faceted approach has a better chance of reducing the ever-growing amount of spam than a solitary solution. And stemming this rising tide is essential if the Internet is to continue to be an effective medium of communication and commerce.

If spam continues to grow, people will rely on their email less and less. Right now, consumers are becoming so frustrated at the junk email bombardment that they delete legitimate commercial email as if it were spam.

This is why so many interested parties, including the Direct Marketing Association, have come around to the view that the federal government can play a meaningful role in stopping spam.

They know that effective federal anti-spam legislation will make it more likely that consumers will read legitimate marketing messages.

I think we can all agree that spammers must not be allowed to bog down the vast potential of email and the Internet.

It is my hope that [we can] stimulate ideas to stop spammers in their tracks. I look forward to . . . working with all of you to bring an end to the current junk email epidemic.

VIEWPOINT

6

"There is a problem in saying that we shall enjoy the freedom to contact or visit companies anytime we like, but they can't contact us."

Regulations Should Not Be Implemented to Reduce Unwanted Spam

Clyde Wayne Crews Jr.

The government should not impose regulations that limit unsolicited commercial e-mail, or spam, argues Clyde Wayne Crews Jr. in the following viewpoint, which was originally given as testimony before the U.S. House of Representatives on May 10, 2001. He contends that spam is a form of free speech and is protected under the First Amendment. According to Crews, regulation of spam will bring unintended negative consequences, such as hindering the growth of small businesses and the Internet. He believes that existing and emerging market forces, not government regulation, can create a solution to unwanted spam. Crews is director of technology studies at the Cato Institute.

As you read, consider the following questions:

1. In what specific circumstances might unsolicited e-mail be a crime, according to Crews?
2. Why is commerce on the Internet critical, according to Crews?
3. In the author's view, how would spam legislation that impedes anonymity be harmful?

Clyde Wayne Crews Jr., testimony before the U.S. House Judiciary Committee, Washington, DC, May 10, 2001.

In the heated debate over the outpouring of unsolicited bulk email, otherwise known as "spam," it's important to remember that not every unsolicited message is evil incarnate. Despite the hysteria, the optimal amount of unsolicited commercial email is not zero. Sometimes, commercial email is friendly or otherwise welcome—yet unsolicited.

Unsolicited commercial mail can be annoying, but it probably tops out as a vice rather than a crime except in rather specific instances, such as when the sender is peddling fraudulent or phony goods, or is impersonating someone else in the message's header information. Or perhaps a sender might be breaking a bulk-mailing contract he has made with an Internet Service provider (ISP).

Laws supposedly designed to halt spam can do more harm than good. . . .

It's not apparent that businesses that are selling legal and legitimate products have any less right to use email than anyone else. The Internet as it exists today is a public, open system and none can legitimately claim a right to exclude others and have the medium regulated on their behalf. However the government must protect citizens against force and fraud.

Problems with Government Regulation

As this testimony argues, with solutions available and improving on the sender, ISP and user side and even hints that the spam problem is stabilizing, legislation is not wise, especially when it's considered that Internet communication itself is still a moving target; email is just one manifestation. Government should not use the novelty of the technology to justify intervention, especially when there's plenty of novelty to come. Conditions are changing every day. We don't have all the answers to the spam problem, and interference now can impede superior solutions to the dilemma that are emerging.

Besides, if the idea is to target the most annoying kinds of spam (LOSE WEIGHT FAST!; MAKE MONEY AT HOME!; XXX!), spam laws simply will not be enforceable. The bad guys will just go offshore, out of the reach of legislation, and the effect of a spam law will simply be to create mischief and regulatory hoops for mainstream companies who typically are not the greatest offenders. Legitimate companies will end up being targeted, with small business likely taking a lot of the brunt of the rules. . . .

Spam is just marketing. And there are different levels of spam "guilt." Spam is much less invasive than door-to-door selling, but we don't outlaw that. It's best to allow people to decide for themselves whether or not to entertain sales pitches. To the extent unsolicited communication is responsible for growth of the Internet and future communications options, hindering unsolicited mail could hamper access for many; a government created digital divide. . . .

Spam clearly remains a problem but it's one ripe for political mischief, as legislation proposed can be more problematic than spam itself. The debate thrives on loaded language, like the word "spam" itself, or in the description of marketers collecting emails as "harvesting." Some seem to detest Internet commerce as a worldview. But commerce and a commercialized Internet are critical to expanding online services, and access itself. . . .

The market is moving toward solutions for a spam problem that may in fact have stabilized. The prospects are good, and legislation intended to target specific areas can have unintended effects that bleed over and hinder superior private solutions as well as online commerce and consumer access to growing online services. It's not enough just to have an aversion to spam, and then feel that's all we need to know. The legislative cure can be worse than the disease. And it can bring a lot of expensive enforcement and litigation costs . . . in the bargain. It's not even clear that all the voices are being heard in the debate. Most small businesses are not on the Internet, and it's not clear that they would have an easy time meeting legislative hurdles. . . .

Impacts of Regulation on Free Speech

Spam is, at bottom, merely advertising. And business speech is still just speech. There is a problem in saying that we shall enjoy the freedom to contact or visit companies anytime we like, but they can't contact us. Even the opt-out requirement . . . can be problematic: does it preclude *all* future contact from a company by email—or just contact about a particular subject or offering? It's certainly fine for consumers to effect complete blackouts from companies if they like. But implementing this with federal legislation appears to be overly heavy handed, and better left to emerging contractual relationships.

Anti-Spam Measures Are Unacceptable

Email is protected speech. There is a fundamental free speech right to be able to send and receive messages, regardless of medium. Unless that right is being abused by a particular individual, that individual must not be restricted. It is unacceptable, then, for anti-spam policies to limit legitimate rights to send or receive email. To the extent that an anti-spam proposal, whether legal or technical, results in such casualties, that proposal is unacceptable.

Electronic Frontier Foundation, October 16, 2001.

Plus, the precedent set would be troublesome: Could advertising restrictions pop up elsewhere, such as on the new Web pop up ads? . . .

Leave Well Enough Alone

Right now the Internet, especially as we sit on the cusp of a revolution in peer-to-peer networking, is one of the only unregulated, open-to-all forms of communication we have. The benefits of leaving it alone, despite problems with some of the "communicators" that populate cyberspace, vastly outweigh the potential costs.

In a way, the spam debate helps illustrate that the underlying crucial Internet debate is really not the one about privacy that gets all the media attention these days. Rather, the real question is whether government will allow individuals to remain anonymous when they actually have the technological means to do so. As strange as it may sound, "spam" and the use of "spamware" are means by which individuals can maintain a cloak of anonymity. . . . For example, Spam Mimic is a Website that disguises a message by making it look like spam so that "sniffers" might be more likely to ignore it.

At the very time the concern is to enhance privacy on the Internet, it's unwise to criminalize uses of software that hide headers, or source and routing information. Consumers may seek these for privacy reasons. Spam legislation that impedes anonymity and individuals' attempts to protect their privacy would be taking away with one hand what government proposes to give with the other. Here, the federal government would be artificially harming privacy, and setting the stage for unnecessary privacy regulations.

This is the kind of unintended consequence that can emerge when governments try to leapfrog the fact that we still have a lot of learning to do. . . .

The Federal Trade Commission already has power to "prosecute fraudulent or misleading commercial emails." States likewise have powers to prosecute fraud. Otherwise, it's better to let existing and emerging market tools address the spam problem because of harmful impacts of legislation on legitimate commercial emails, emerging Internet communications methods and free speech.

Government should not grant ISP's a top-down right to block, with immunity. While private efforts to block spam do not constitute state action, government-sanctioned blockage arguably crosses that line and violates free speech. . . .

The government can't stop spam. In the final analysis, the market will have to do the heavy lifting. Regulation now is likely to simply harm legitimate commerce. In trying to make life difficult for unsolicited mail, it is all too easy to make it difficult for solicited mail, too.

Periodical Bibliography

The following articles have been selected to supplement the diverse views presented in this chapter.

Broadcasting & Cable	"Get Some Guts," March 1, 2004.
Robert Corn-Revere	"The First Amendment and the Electronic Media," www.firstamendmentcenter.org.
Clyde Wayne Crews Jr.	"Government Can't Protect Kids from Porn—but Parents Can," *San Diego Union-Tribune*, May 17, 2002.
E. Edwards	"The Limits of Internet Filtering," *Washington Post*, December 16, 2002.
Mike Gilbert	"Spam Is Not Free Speech and Should Be Banned," *Seattle Times*, December 22, 2003.
Linda Greenhouse	"Sides Debate Web Access in Libraries," *New York Times*, March 6, 2003.
Kenneth Jost	"Libraries and the Internet," *CQ Researcher*, June 1, 2001.
Erkki Likanen and Patrick J. Leahy	"Continents Clash on Content," *New York Times*, April 18, 2001.
Mary Minow	"Who Pays for Free Speech? The Cost of Defending the First Amendment Is Diverting Scarce Resources from Library Services," *American Libraries*, February 2003.
Geoffrey Nunberg	"Machines Make Moral Judgments, Selectively; Software May Block St. Sebastian, but Not a Penthouse Centerfold," *New York Times*, March 9, 2003.
John Schwartz	"Internet Filters Block Many Useful Sites, Study Finds," *New York Times*, December 11, 2002.
Laura Sullivan	"Administration Wages War on Pornography," *Baltimore Sun*, April 6, 2004.
Shyam Sunder	"A Free Market Solution to Spam," www.cato.org, February 27, 2004.

CHAPTER 3

Has America's War on Terrorism Led to Increased Censorship?

Chapter Preface

In late 2001 Paramount Studios was preparing to release its latest movie: *The Sum of All Fears*. In this Hollywood thriller, a terrorist group detonates a nuclear bomb in a crowded football stadium in Maryland, killing thousands of people. Right before the release of the movie, however, on September 11, 2001, a real-life terrorist attack occurred. Al Qaeda terrorists hijacked four planes and crashed them into the World Trade Center in New York and the Pentagon in Washington, D.C.; a fourth plane crashed into a field in Pennsylvania. More than three thousand people died in this nonfictional attack—the worst terrorist attack ever to occur in the United States.

Americans were surprised and hurt by the attack on their country. The entertainment industry reacted with a plethora of last-minute changes to its lineup. Paramount postponed the release of *The Sum of All Fears* due to its terrorist theme. Many other movies dealing with terrorist-related content were similarly postponed or canceled. In addition, dozens of movies, television shows, and commercials were edited to remove terrorist-related subject matter, including images of the World Trade Center towers. Blockbuster Video placed labels on some rental videos to warn of terrorist-themed content. While some people viewed these actions as merely a necessary expression of sensitivity to the events of September 11, many others decried them as Hollywood censorship.

Indeed, the entertainment industry's reaction to the terrorist attacks has caused widespread controversy. Producers defended their decisions to alter or remove movie and television content, arguing that in light of the attacks, it was inappropriate to portray these themes; they believed that audiences did not want to see them. According to writer Joe Morgenstern of the *Wall Street Journal*, it would be inappropriate to make entertainment mirroring the terrible loss of life that occurred on September 11. He argues that, "There are times when fiction films collide with reality and must be judged accordingly. The last thing we need is entertainment that evokes the horror and then trivializes it with cheesy heroics."

However, rather than seeing Hollywood's actions as being sensitive to tragic events, critics interpreted them as unnecessary censorship. Journalist Adam Groves argues, "The Hollywood censorship machine sprang into action almost immediately [after the attacks]." Critics such as Groves believe that this censorship is a dangerous threat to freedom of expression in American society. He warns that "if this sort of cowardly censorship is what we can expect in times of crisis, then the harsh reality is that it will very likely only get worse."

Hollywood, of course, is not the only entity accused of infringing on free speech after the September 11 attacks and the subsequent war on terrorism. Critics have accused the media and the federal government of engaging in censorship as well. The authors in the following chapter offer some opinions on this controversy as they debate whether censorship has increased as a result of America's ongoing battle against terrorism.

"*The Constitution guarantees that Americans have the right to read books, write books, and express their opinions. Even when the ideas expressed are unpopular.*"

The Patriot Act Has Led to Increased Censorship in the United States

Eleanor J. Bader

Immediately following the September 11, 2001, terrorist attacks, U.S. lawmakers passed the Patriot Act, which enhances law enforcement powers. In the following viewpoint Eleanor J. Bader argues that the Patriot Act violates the right of Americans to freely express their opinions. The government can now monitor what library users read, contends Bader, which violates the First Amendment right to expression free from government interference. In addition, she points out, the act discourages people from seeking information about Islam and the Middle East. Bader is a freelance writer and teacher.

As you read, consider the following questions:

1. According to Bader, the Patriot Act has given new surveillance powers to the executive branch. What are some examples of these powers?
2. What does the gag provision of the Patriot Act mandate, according to Bader?

Eleanor J. Bader, "Thought Police, Big Brother May Be Watching What You Read," *In These Times*, vol. 26, November 25, 2002, p. 3. Copyright © 2002 by *In These Times*. Reproduced by permission.

Within days of the September 11 [2001, terrorist attacks], the police and FBI were besieged with tips informing them that several suspects—including one who fit [September 11 hijacker] Mohammed Atta's description—had used public libraries in Hollywood Beach and Delray Beach, Florida, to surf the Internet. Shortly thereafter, a federal grand jury ordered library staff to submit all user records to law enforcement.

Monitoring Reading Material

The order began a pattern of government requests for information about citizens' reading material that has increased dramatically since last October's [2001] passage of the USA Patriot Act, which amended 15 federal statutes, including laws governing criminal procedure, computer fraud, foreign intelligence, wire-tapping, immigration and privacy. The act gives the government a host of new powers, including the ability to scrutinize what a person reads or purchases.

According to a University of Illinois study of 1,020 libraries conducted during the first two months of 2002, government sources asked 85 university and public libraries—8.3 percent of those queried—for information on patrons following the attacks. More detail is unknown since divulging specific information violates provisions of the legislation.

"The act grants the executive branch unprecedented, and largely unchecked, surveillance powers," says attorney Nancy Chang, author of *Silencing Political Dissent*, "including the enhanced ability to track e-mail and Internet usage, obtain sensitive personal records from third parties, monitor financial transactions and conduct nationwide roving wiretaps."

In fact, a court can now allow a wiretap to follow a suspect wherever he or she goes, including a public library or bookstore. That's right: Booksellers can also be targeted. What's more, the government is no longer required to demonstrate "probable cause" when requesting records. "FBI and police used to have to show probable cause that a person had committed a crime when requesting materials," says Chris Finan, president of the American Booksellers Foundation for Free Expression (ABFFE).

"Now, under Section 215 of the Patriot Act," Finan con-

Cagle. © 2002 by Cagle Cartoons, Inc. Reproduced by permission.

tinues, "it is possible for them to investigate a person who is not suspected of criminal activity, but who may have some connection to a person [who is]. Worse . . . there is a gag provision barring bookstores or libraries from telling anyone—including the suspect—about the investigation. Violators of the gag order can go to jail."

Outrage and Concern

Members of Congress, as well as librarians, booksellers and ordinary citizens, have expressed outrage and concern over the Orwellian[1] reach of the law. On June 12 [2002], the House Judiciary Committee sent a 12-page letter to the Justice Department requesting hard data on the number of subpoenas issued to booksellers and libraries since last October [2001]. Two months later, on August 19, Assistant Attorney General

1. state-enforced conformity through indoctrination and fear; based on George Orwell's novel *1984*

Daniel J. Bryant responded. The figures are "confidential," he wrote, and will only be shared with the House Intelligence Committee. The Judiciary Committee told Bryant the response was unsatisfactory. Finan reports that everyone is "waiting to see what the committee will do next."

Meanwhile, the ABFFE has joined a coalition of booksellers and libraries to denounce Section 215. They have also signed onto a Freedom of Information Act request for information on both the number and content of subpoenas issued. To date, there has been no response to their entreaty; though such responses are required by law, they can often take months or even years to complete.[2]

But community activists, librarians and publishers have joined forces to publicize the threat that the act poses to free speech, privacy and civil liberties. The American Library Association [ALA], a national alliance of library staff, issued a statement in early 2002 affirming their position: "Librarians do not police what library users read or access in the library. Libraries ensure the freedom to read, to view, to speak, and to participate."

Though the ALA has agreed to cooperate with federal requests within the framework of state law, it has warned local branches not to create or retain unnecessary records, and trained staff to read subpoenas carefully before providing unnecessary information.

Taking a Toll on Constitutional Rights

Despite this modicum of defiance, everyone agrees that Section 215 has begun to exact a toll. "Right after 9/11, Americans seemed eager to learn more about the world," says Larry Siems, director of International Programs at the PEN American Center. "They were reading, buying and checking out books on Islam. . . . But the administration's overall approach discourages people from seeking information. It is counterproductive. We end up with a society that is more isolated, less able to respond to the rest of the world."

In addition, he states, the Constitution guarantees that

---

2. In 2003 the Justice Department revealed that no subpoenas had been issued to libraries or booksellers. Activists, librarians, and publishers maintained that the Patriot Act was still a threat to freedom.

Americans have the right to read books, write books, and express their opinions. Even when the ideas expressed are unpopular—even when they're downright unpatriotic or seditious—the government should not be in the business of prohibiting them. Indeed, he cautions, a distinction between acts and ideas is imperative.

Finan and Chang agree, and they are doing their best to ensure that the Patriot Act fades away in October 2005, when it is set to expire. "At the very least," Finan concludes, "we want changes in sections like 215, to exempt libraries and bookstores from scrutiny."

"No one believes in our First Amendment civil liberties more than [the Bush] administration. . . . We seek a war for justice that reflects the noblest ideals and highest standards set by the United States Constitution."

The Patriot Act Has Not Led to Unnecessary Censorship in the United States

John Ashcroft

The Patriot Act, which enhances federal law enforcement powers, was passed immediately after the September 11, 2001, terrorist attacks. In the following viewpoint, former U.S. attorney general John Ashcroft dismisses claims that the Patriot Act has led to increased censorship in the United States. The law enforcement community is fighting to protect freedom in America, he argues, and the Patriot Act simply helps it do its job more effectively. With the aid of the act, contends Ashcroft, both freedom and security have been preserved.

As you read, consider the following questions:

1. Even if the Justice Department was interested in tracking the reading habits of Americans, why would this be impossible, according to Ashcroft?
2. According to the author, what requirements must be met before a law enforcement official can obtain library records?
3. How many terrorist suspects has the United States captured in its fight against terrorism, as cited by Ashcroft?

John Ashcroft, "The Proven Tactics in the Fight Against Crime," address, Washington, DC, September 15, 2003.

The genius of our system of government is that in America, we believe that it is the people who grant the government its powers. We believe that it is the people's values that should be imposed on Washington—not Washington's values on the people. . . .

Unfortunately, at this moment, Washington is involved in a debate where hysteria threatens to obscure the most important issues.

Hysteria

If you were to listen to some in Washington, you might believe the hysteria behind this claim: "Your local library has been surrounded by the FBI." Agents are working round-the-clock. Like [in] the *X-Files* [television show], they are dressed in raincoats, dark suits, and sporting sunglasses. They stop patrons and librarians and interrogate everyone. . . . In a dull monotone they ask every person exiting the library, "Why were you at the library? What were you reading? Did you see anything suspicious?"

According to these breathless reports and baseless hysteria, some have convinced the American Library Association that under the bipartisan Patriot Act, the FBI is not fighting terrorism. Instead, agents are checking how far you have gotten on the latest Tom Clancy novel.

Now you may have thought with all this hysteria and hyperbole, something had to be wrong. Do we at the Justice Department really care what you are reading? No.

The law enforcement community has no interest in your reading habits. Tracking reading habits would betray our high regard for the First Amendment. And even if someone in the government wanted to do so, it would represent an impossible workload and a waste of law enforcement resources.

The fact is that our laws are very particular and very demanding. There are strict legal requirements. A federal judge must first determine that there is an existing investigation of an international terrorist or spy, or a foreign intelligence investigation into a non-U.S. person, and that the business records being sought are relevant to that investigation. Without meeting these legal requirements, obtaining business records, including library records, is not even an option.

With only 11,000 FBI agents in the entire country, it is simply ridiculous to think we could or would track what citizens are reading. I am not in a position to know, but according to the American Library Association there are more than 117,400 libraries in the United States. The American Library Association tells me that Americans visit our nation's libraries more than one billion times a year—1,146,284,000, to be exact. While there, they check out nearly two billion books a year—1,713,967,000, to be precise.

The hysteria is ridiculous. Our job is not.

Protecting Liberty in America

It is the solemn belief of the United States Department of Justice that the first and primary responsibility of government is: to preserve the lives and protect the liberty of the people.

No one believes in our First Amendment civil liberties more than this administration. It is what we are fighting for in this war against tyranny. On my watch, we seek a war for justice that reflects the noblest ideals and highest standards set by the United States Constitution. I would not support or invite any change that might restructure or endanger our individual liberties and personal freedoms.

It would be a tragedy if the hysteria surrounding certain aspects of our war against terror were to obscure the important evidence that the Department of Justice has protected the lives and liberties of the citizenry, and not just in the very real world of anti-terrorism.

The American people deserve to know that violent crime has plunged to its lowest point in 30 years.

Thanks to this President's leadership and the work of the justice community, these numbers almost speak for themselves. But for the crime rate to hit a 30-year low, we had to focus on and drive down almost every category of crime. . . .

Prevention Rooted in Constitutional Liberties

Preventing crime by punishing criminals gets results. By enhancing cooperation, passing tougher laws, and enacting tough penalties, we have driven down crime. These same tactics have been deployed in the war on terror and they are the reason we prevented any terrorist attack [after the

Fighting a New Type of Threat

We're now facing the first war of the 21st century. It's a different kind of war. . . . Now the enemy hides in caves. They lurk in the shadows of the world. They will strike and kill innocent citizens without any conscience, because they have no conscience.

So the fundamental charge before us all in positions of responsibility is, how do we deal with the threat? . . .

Part of the problem we face was that there was laws and bureaucratic mind-sets that prevented the sharing of information. And so, besides setting up the Homeland Security Department and beefing up our air travel security, and making sure that we now fingerprint at the borders and take those fingerprints, by the way, and compare to a master log of fingerprints of terrorists and known criminals, to make sure people coming into our country are the right people coming into our country. I mean, we do a lot of things. But we change law, as well, to allow the FBI . . . to be able to share information within the FBI. . . .

The way I viewed it, if I can just put it in simple terms, is that one part of the FBI couldn't tell the other part of the FBI vital information because of law. And the CIA and the FBI couldn't talk. Now, these are people charged with gathering information about threats to the country; yet they couldn't share the information. And right after September the 11th [2001] the Congress wisely acted, said, this doesn't make any sense. If we can't get people talking, how can we act? We're charged with the security of the country, first responders are charged with the security of the country, and if we can't share information between vital agencies, we're not going to be able to do our job. And they acted.

So the first thing I want you to think about is, when you hear Patriot Act, is that we changed the law and the bureaucratic mind-set to allow for the sharing of information. It's vital.

George W. Bush, April 20, 2004.

September 11, 2001, terrorist attacks].

In every corner of the nation and at every level of government, the justice community has worked together, shared information, and struck at terrorist cells who would do us harm. Law enforcement has embraced the tools and spirit of the Patriot Act by communicating information, coordinating their efforts, and cooperating toward our integrated strategy of preventing terrorism. This has meant smarter, better-focused law enforcement—law enforcement that targets terrorists and secures our borders, letting hard-working immigrants and free trade prosper in a nation blessed by freedom.

In fact, the results of our anti-terrorism efforts are just as impressive and just as undeniable as our success in driving crime to a 30-year low.

All told, two-thirds of [terrorist group] Al Qaeda's senior leadership have been captured or killed. And more than 3,000 suspected terrorists have been arrested in countries around the world. Many more have met a different fate.

Specifically:

• We have dismantled terrorist operations in New York, Michigan, Washington State, Oregon, and North Carolina;

• We have brought criminal charges against 262 individuals;

• 143 individuals have been convicted or pled guilty, including shoe-bomber Richard Reid, "American Taliban" John Walker Lindh, six members of the Buffalo cell, and two members of the Detroit cell;[1]

• We have deported more than 515 individuals with links to the September 11th [2001, terrorist attacks] investigation; and

• We have stopped more than $200 million from funding terrorist groups.

This nation has never asked more of the men and women of law enforcement. And law enforcement has never achieved more than these past few years.

At every level of law enforcement, in every area of fighting crime, we have committed ourselves to a new strategy—a strategy of prevention. It is rooted in our Constitutional liberties, built on communication and cooperation and driven by the courage and integrity of the men and women of law enforcement. From the FBI in Washington to the local cop with his feet on the street, we owe our thanks for their hard work and respect for freedom and the law.

---

1. British citizen Richard Reid attempted to destroy a passenger airliner by igniting explosives hidden in his shoes. John Walker Lindh is an American citizen who was captured in Afghanistan while fighting for the Islamist Taliban there. The Buffalo and Detroit cells were Al Qaeda terrorist groups.

3

"In a nation that haughtily markets itself to the rest of the world as a haven for free speech, why is dissent regarded as unpatriotic, as un-American, during times of crisis?"

The Right to Dissent Has Been Threatened in the War on Terrorism

Simon Houpt

Dissent in the United States has been quashed as Americans unite to support the government's war on terrorism, contends Simon Houpt in the following viewpoint. According to Houpt, both the media and the government have attempted to silence opinions regarded as unpatriotic. He cautions that by attempting to censor opinions critical of America, the nation is in danger of sacrificing freedom. Houpt is a columnist for the Toronto *Globe and Mail* daily newspaper.

As you read, consider the following questions:
1. Why did Susan Sontag receive threats following the September 11, 2001, terrorist attacks, as cited by Houpt?
2. Why was newspaper editor Tom Gutting fired, according to the author?
3. What two historical examples does Houpt give of dissent being quashed in the United States?

Simon Houpt, "The War on Dissent," *Globe and Mail*, October 6, 2001, p. R1. Copyright © 2001 by Globe Interactive, a division of Bell Globemedia Publishing, Inc. Reproduced by permission.

When two airliners smashed into the twin towers of the World Trade Center [on September 11, 2003], writer Susan Sontag was in Berlin, glued to CNN, the only U.S. newscast she could receive. In the 40 hours that followed, she watched a parade of military and political experts stroll across the screen, apparently united in their convictions over the causes of and solutions to the terrorist attacks.

"It was amazing: To see Richard Holbrooke, Madeleine Albright, Henry Kissinger—they all can't stand each other—to see them all come on and say exactly the same thing? It made me laugh!" Sontag said in an interview. "So I said: Why can't there be some debate?"

Adding Some Debate

Stuck in Berlin by the closure of American airports, Sontag was asked by *The New Yorker* to contribute to the magazine's first Talk of the Town section published after the attacks. This is what she wrote: "The unanimity of the sanctimonious, reality-concealing rhetoric spouted by American officials and media commentators in recent days seems, well, unworthy of a mature democracy."

Noting that U.S. President George W. Bush had said the terrorists were cowards, she submitted, "if the word 'cowardly' is to be used, it might be more aptly applied to those who kill from beyond the range of retaliation, high in the sky, than to those willing to die themselves in order to kill others . . . whatever may be said of the perpetrators of Tuesday's slaughter, they were not cowards."

The magazine hit newsstands in New York on Sept. 17. [2001]. That night, 4,000 kilometres across the country in a Los Angeles television studio, *Politically Incorrect* [television show] host Bill Maher began his first show after the attacks with a tribute to one of those killed the previous week. Conservative pundit Barbara Olson had been en route from Washington to L.A. to promote her new book on the show when her plane was flown into the Pentagon. Sitting a few feet from a seat left empty in memory of Olson, Maher echoed Sontag's words.

"We have been the cowards, lobbing cruise missiles from 2,000 miles away, that's cowardly," he said. "Staying in the airplane when it hits the building, say what you want about it, that's not cowardly."

Yikes. Maher is a contract provocateur, willing to say just about anything for ratings, and in the past advertisers have jauntily supported his schoolyard taunts. Coming so soon after the Sept. 11 attacks, however, his comments were considered hurtful and unbecoming for a man employed by ABC Networks, which is owned by Disney.

The day after the broadcast, FedEx pulled its ads in protest, followed by Sears Roebuck. As Maher tried desperately to spin his words, TV stations around the country began pulling *Politically Incorrect* from their airwaves. Even after Maher offered an outright apology, as many as 17 stations briefly dropped the show.

In No Mood for Dissent

It was becoming apparent that the American public was in no mood to hear any criticism of the country or its leader.

Sontag was back in New York by this time, receiving anonymous threats and not so anonymous attacks for voicing her opinion. The *New Yorker* offices were deluged with letters of complaint and Sontag was pilloried in the pages of dozens of newspapers and political weeklies by the usual cast of curmudgeonly columnists. A senior editor at *The New Republic* grouped Sontag in with [terrorist leader] Osama bin Laden and [former Iraqi president] Saddam Hussein, characterizing her as someone who wants America's global power to be dismantled.

On the Fox News Channel, which is owned by Rupert Murdoch's News Corp., a retired U.S. Army colonel suggested that any criticism of America's war on terrorism might be considered treasonous.

Less than one week after the World Trade Center attack, posters appeared in bus shelters and telephone booths around the country with the vow: "United We Stand." Millions of flags now [in 2001] flutter from lawns, rooftops, window ledges and car aerials. In words and deeds, Americans are declaring: "United We Speak."

Dissent has all but disappeared.

"It's all preposterous," Sontag said. . . . "I'm stunned by

the reaction, because it tells something about the mood of the country. I find that prevalence of group-think absolutely extraordinary. I find it extraordinary that the press secretary of the President of the United States would say people have to watch what they say as well as what they do. That sends chills up and down my spine. If I take it seriously as a turn in the spirit of the country, I would be much more alarmed, but I hope that's not true.

"I just said something elementary and old-fashioned American. It's very depressing to see how scared people are to say anything except to read from this script. If I think that it is the beginning of a new age in which essentially freedom of speech is only something we afford in prosperous and calm times, then I would say that is the end of the United States of America being a country that I admire."

Suppression in Times of Crisis

Sontag might not be interested in hearing, then, that Americans have always been quick to sacrifice freedom of speech in anxious times.

"It's part of the landscape," said Thomas McCoy, a law professor at Vanderbilt University who specializes in the First Amendment. "When there's a national crisis, particularly a war situation, you find widespread attempts to suppress unpopular or inconvenient viewpoints."

The strongest condemnation of unpopular viewpoints in the wake of the Sept. 11 attacks came from presidential spokesman Ari Fleischer, who chastised Maher from the bully pulpit of the White House briefing room.

"All Americans . . . need to watch what they say, watch what they do," said Fleischer. ". . . This is not a time for remarks like that. It never is." The chilling effect of his comment wasn't diminished by the fact that he was also referring to a racist remark by a Louisiana Republican congressman.

While the First Amendment prevents government from clamping down on critical speech, private companies are free to censure their employees at whim. Nothing in law precludes ABC from cancelling *Politically Incorrect* if the network suddenly decides Maher's politically incorrect speech is more a liability than an asset.

If they choose, advertisers may back out of sponsoring the publication of opinions with which they or their audience disagree, as FedEx did.

Maher's comments brought "numerous general complaints," according to FedEx spokesman Jim McCluskey. "There's an environment there where words should be guarded carefully and there should be appropriate sensitivity to circumstances as they exist." McCluskey offered this odd assessment of a core American value: "I don't think freedom of speech is really at issue. It's just the nature in which free speech is used.". . .

Media Censorship of Dissent

In widely publicized incidents, two other writers were fired last month [September 2001] after they criticized the actions George W. Bush took in the early hours after the terrorist attacks.

Dan Guthrie, a columnist and copy editor at *The Daily Courier* in the small town of Grants Pass, Ore., said he was fired after writing that Bush "skedaddled" and hid out "in a Nebraska hole," waiting for the danger to pass. At the *Texas City Sun*, city editor Tom Gutting was fired for voicing similar sentiments. The paper's editor and publisher Les Daughtry Jr. announced Gutting's dismissal in a front-page apology.

"Tom's column was so offensive to me personally that I had a hard time getting all the way through it, and in fact, still feel ill from its effects as I write this," Daughtry wrote. He concluded: "May God bless President George W. Bush and other leaders. And God bless America!"

Newly wary of the sensibilities of their audiences and the pressing need to maintain sources as the pipeline for information gets squeezed, many journalists are holding back from asking tough questions of the administration. Immediately after the attacks, some news anchors and many local reporters donned red-white-and-blue flag pins, while a number of networks replaced their usual logos with American flags or red-white-and-blue renditions of the logos. A senior vice-president at the Fox News Channel said the network was proud to fly a waving American flag on screen.

"I'd sure prefer that to a hammer and sickle, I'll tell you that," Rick Moody said, as if those were the only two choices. "I think that there's some patriotism on camera now, and I think inasmuch as TV news often reflects America's mood at any given moment, that's what it's doing now."

To be sure, the media's goose-stepping disappoints some Americans.

"Our media, it's so pathetic and embarrassing," said the film director and left-wing rabble-rouser Michael Moore. Normally a frequent guest on cable-news shows, Moore says he hasn't been called to appear on any American TV stations since the attacks.

Importance of Debate in Times of Crisis

Engaging in debate over public policy and giving serious consideration to unpopular opinions that question prevailing wisdom—even in times of national crisis—are high forms of civic engagement and patriotism.

Joel Benin, *Los Angeles Times*, December 30, 2001.

"I've been called by the CBC [Canadian Broadcasting Corporation], BBC [British Broadcasting Corporation], ABC in Australia," he said in an interview. "I've been on the nightly newscast of every Western country, practically, and I've not had a single call from the American networks. . . . Because I'm going to go on there and say the things they don't want to hear. I'm going to be off message. I'm not going to sing with the chorus. And the media is part of the chorus now. They're wearing their ribbons and they're not being objective journalists and they're not presenting all sides. . . ."

No Tolerance for Unpatriotic Speech

"My problems pale in comparison to [the victims of the attacks and their families], so I'm not whining about it. I'm just saying this is a time when writers and artists need to really act with courage, stand up, say the things that they need to say, and trust that there's enough of the American public that will hear what you're saying."

On Sept. 12 [2001], Moore posted a diary entry on his Web site, MichaelMoore.com, suggesting that perhaps the

U.S. didn't have the moral authority to decry the activities of terrorists.

"We abhor terrorism—unless we're the ones doing the terrorizing. We paid and trained and armed a group of terrorists in Nicaragua in the 1980s who killed more than 30,000 civilians. That was OUR work. You and me. Thirty thousand murdered civilians and who the hell even remembers! We fund a lot of oppressive regimes that have killed a lot of innocent people, and we never let the human suffering THAT causes interrupt our day one single bit."

The response? Moore says his site is getting more than one million hits per week.

"People are desperate," he says. "They're looking for alternative sources of information." Since the attacks, he has received more than 70,000 e-mails. Most of them are supportive but he acknowledges that many are not. "The tone of the hate mail that I've received is as vicious and violent as it's ever been toward me, in terms of threatening to kill me and do other things to me."

Clearly, the American people are in no mood for speech that might challenge their certainties. Thursday night on *Politically Incorrect*, political cartoonist Dan Rall was roundly booed when he reminded the audience that George W. Bush's victory in November's presidential election was still unresolved.[1] "That's so Sept. 10th," scolded a patronizing Bill Maher. "It really is."

Tradition of Clamping Down on Dissent

The impulse to clamp down on critical speech isn't new. In 1918, with American troops dying in Europe, socialist Eugene Debs was charged and convicted under the war-time Espionage Act for protesting the First World War. He was sentenced to 10 years in prison and disenfranchised, losing his citizenship for life. (Debs still managed to run for president from prison on the Socialist ticket and earn about one million votes.)

---

1. The validity of the Florida vote in the election was disputed. After Al Gore conceded the election, Bush became president; however, some people disputed the appointment.

During the Red Scare of the 1940s and '50s, which Senator Joseph McCarthy masterfully exploited, public fear of Communists in America was so strong that the Harvard sociologist Samuel Stouffer found two-thirds of people polled in 1954 said a Communist shouldn't be permitted to speak. Sixty per cent said an atheist shouldn't be permitted to speak.

"The Cold War was viewed as a major national crisis," said Prof. McCoy, "so any dissenters were being dragged before the House Un-American Activities Committee and fired from their jobs in Hollywood and universities.

"It just seems that when we feel the need to pull together against a common enemy, our normal American tolerance for dissent is a casualty of that felt need to pull together."

In a nation that haughtily markets itself to the rest of the world as a haven for free speech, why is dissent regarded as unpatriotic, as un-American, during times of crisis?

Moore thinks it's something in the national character of Americans. He is censoring himself in publishing comments that might prove hurtful to the twin-tower victims—one of his friends was on the plane that slammed into the south tower—but he is trying to understand how the tragedy occurred.

"I still can't get out of my head how three guys with box cutters keep 90 people at bay. And yet I don't want to blame the victims for not doing anything. But what is it in us—they cut one person's throat, we watch one person die and then we're paralyzed with fear? What is that?". . .

Prof. McCoy doesn't understand it, either, but he can appreciate the inherent irony. "In the course of banding together to defend what we believe in, we have a tendency to sacrifice one of the core beliefs that we're defending. That is ironic, but it is an observable fact."

"Our First Amendment rights continue to be strong. Just as strong are the consequences for using those First Amendment rights without first using our brain."

The Right to Dissent Has Not Been Threatened in the War on Terrorism

Bobby Eberle

The First Amendment right to political dissent has not been threatened in America's war on terrorism, argues Bobby Eberle in the following viewpoint. Celebrities and others have the right to freely express their dissent, he maintains. The criticism and lack of sympathy these dissenters have received should not be interpreted as a loss of freedom, contends Eberle; it is simply a result of the fact that most Americans do support the war on terrorism and thus disagree with these protesters. Eberle is president and chief executive officer of GOPUSA, a company that provides news, information, and commentary on current events.

As you read, consider the following questions:

1. What does Eberle believe is the real reason that Tim Robbins and his wife were not welcome at the Baseball Hall of Fame event?
2. Why might Americans sometimes refrain from exercising their First Amendment right to freedom of speech, according to the author?
3. How are many celebrities out of touch with public opinion, as cited by Eberle?

Bobby Eberle, "Celebs Speak Their Mind and Expect Others to Keep Quiet," *Insight on the News*, vol. 19, May 13, 2003, pp. 50–51. Copyright © 2003 by News World Communications, Inc. All rights reserved. Reproduced by permission.

S ince the adoption of the Bill of Rights into the U.S. Constitution, there have been few tenets as reliable as our freedom of speech. On playgrounds across the country, children pour forth with epithets such as "pigface" and "goof ball." When told by peers to be quiet, the standard response is: "It's a free country." The target of the verbal barrage would then respond in kind.

Criticism from adults works in much the same way, or at least it did until we were given the Hollywood interpretation of the First Amendment. According to Hollywood, freedom of speech (when used by a "celebrity") also implies freedom from criticism.

Celebrity Criticism of the War on Terrorism

On April 15 [2003], actor Tim Robbins spoke at the National Press Club in Washington and said that a "chill wind is blowing in this nation," referring to the repercussions he says are being felt by people who spoke out against the war [on terrorism]. "A message is being sent through the White House and its allies in talk radio and Clear Channel [Communications Inc.] and Cooperstown [the town in New York where the Baseball Hall of Fame is located]. If you oppose this administration, there can and will be ramifications," Robbins said.

Robbins goes on to say, "Every day, the airwaves are filled with warnings, veiled and unveiled threats, spewed invective and hatred directed at any voice of dissent. And the public, like so many relatives and friends that I saw this weekend, sit in mute opposition and fear."

Robbins, like many on the liberal left, just doesn't get it. For him, it is perfectly fine to exercise his First Amendment rights to criticize the war with Iraq, President George W. Bush and any number of conservative policies just as long as he is not criticized in return. How dare anyone dispute his claims!

In his speech, Robbins goes as far as saying that he and his "wife," [actress] Susan Sarandon, "were told that both we and the First Amendment were not welcome at the Baseball Hall of Fame [for an event celebrating the anniversary of the film *Bull Durham*]." This comment would be laughable if it

Majority of Americans Support War Against Iraq

Do you think the U.S. made the right decision or the wrong decision in going to war against Iraq?

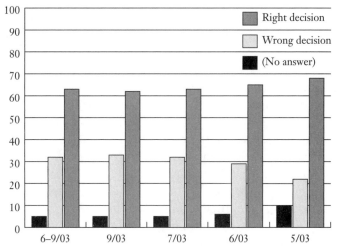

As you may know, President [George W.] Bush did not get UN Security Council authorization to invade, but decided to invade Iraq nonetheless. How do you feel about this decision?

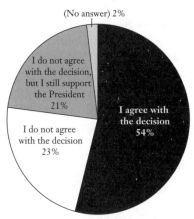

Program on International Policy Attitudes, October 2, 2003.

weren't so scary. Apparently, Robbins and Sarandon find it offensive that the organizers of the Baseball Hall of Fame would exercise their First Amendment rights to say what they want to say and host the kind of event that they want to host. Although it might seem unlikely to some, perhaps the organizers of the Baseball Hall of Fame wanted their event actually to focus on baseball.

Robbins again shows his arrogance when he talks about a friend of his in the music business. "A famous middle-aged rock 'n' roller called me last week to thank me for speaking out against the war, only to go on to tell me that he could not speak himself because he fears repercussions from Clear Channel. 'They promote our concerts appearances,' he said. 'They own most of the [radio] stations that play our music. I can't come out against this war,'" Robbins reported.

Statements such as these demonstrate that many liberal "celebrities" live in an isolated fantasy world. Although Robbins' friends might see that people sometimes are held accountable for what they say, many on the left do not. Many not only feel they can say anything they want and not be criticized for it, they also feel that their words and actions do not have consequences.

First Amendment Right

Yes, we have a First Amendment right to freedom of speech. But, as often as we sometimes want to say it, how many of us actually tell our boss to go jump in a lake? How many of us would actually say "yes" when asked by our wife or girl-friend, "Do I look fat to you?" Why not? Because words are not empty. Words have meaning. Expressing thoughts as spoken words implies a willingness to face the consequences that could happen as a result. In other words, if you can't take the heat, don't open your mouth.

Most Hollywood executives hope that the films they make will be accepted by audiences and make them money. Their motivating factor is the bottom line. So, when faced with circumstances that may affect their bottom line, who can blame them for not taking corrective actions? Who can blame them? The "celebrities" can.

With the public outraged by statements from the likes of [actors and actresses] Janeane Garofalo, Martin Sheen and Sarandon, it seems quite logical that film executives would not cast that trio in a feature and honestly think it would be a box-office hit. When faced with thousands of angry phone calls about the [music group] Dixie Chicks, Clear Channel stations could do one of two things: ignore the deluge of calls from its audience or stop playing the Dixie Chicks.[1] In a simple act of protecting its bottom line, Clear Channel chose to pull the songs. Fortunately, Clear Channel seems as much motivated by patriotism as by economics, but the point is that its actions were justified simply from an economic perspective.

The cries of "conspiracy" by the left about being black-listed for their anti-war/anti-Bush comments also show a complete lack of ability to grasp public opinion. It is not a conspiracy when 80 percent of the people agree that the war to remove [former Iraqi president] Saddam Hussein is a good thing. It is not a conspiracy when phone lines are flooded with callers complaining about the Dixie Chicks criticizing President [George W.] Bush on foreign soil during a war. The majority of Americans support Bush and the war with Iraq, and for these "celebrities" to be surprised when they receive criticism shows just how out of touch they are.

The Hollywood celebrities on the left think they can do or say whatever they please and face no criticism or consequences. It's time for them to wake up and join the real world. Until then, our First Amendment rights continue to be strong. Just as strong are the consequences for using those First Amendment rights without first using our brain.

1. In March 2003, Dixie Chicks member Natalie Maines stated at a concert in London that she was ashamed that U.S. president George W. Bush came from her home state of Texas.

"Occupying authority chief L. Paul Bremer III placed controls on [Iraqi Media Network] content and clamped down on the independent media in Iraq."

The U.S. Occupation of Iraq Has Resulted in Iraqi Media Censorship

Alex Gourevitch

Rather than promote free media expression in Iraq, U.S. occupying forces have actually stifled it, contends Alex Gourevitch in the following viewpoint. According to Gourevitch, because of the desire to prevent anti-Americanism in Iraq, Iraqi media content on the U.S.-run Iraqi Media Network, and on Iraqi-run stations, has been censored by U.S. forces. The result has been a degradation of both the quality and the credibility of media content in Iraq. Gourevitch is a graduate student at Columbia University, and was a writing fellow for the year 2002–2003 at *American Prospect*, a monthly magazine committed to the preservation of democracy.

As you read, consider the following questions:

1. According to the author, why did the Coalition Provisional Authority find itself "between a rock and a hard place" in attempts to oversee the media in postwar Iraq?
2. Why did journalism at the Iraqi Media Network lose its credibility, as cited by Gourevitch?
3. What examples does the author give of censorship of Iraqi media?

Alex Gourevitch, "Exporting Censorship to Iraq," *The American Prospect*, vol. 14, October 2003, p. 34. Copyright © 2003 by The American Prospect, Inc., 5 Broad St., Boston, MA 02109. All rights reserved. Reproduced by permission.

From the start, problems small and large plagued the Pentagon's media project in Iraq. The Iraqi Media Network (IMN), as it is known, is an American-run outfit contracted by the Pentagon to put out news after [Iraqi leader] Saddam Hussein's fall. Its mission was twofold: to be both a PBS [Public Broadcasting Service]-style broadcaster and a means for the occupying authorities to communicate with Iraqis. But getting going wasn't easy. There were bombed-out facilities to reconstruct, transmitters to build, and a staff to hire and rehire when many left for better wages as interpreters or translators. Tapes didn't match with recording machines; recording machines didn't match with broadcasting equipment. There were power outages and battery shortages, and no money to buy new programming. "We were even using the videotape collection of [Hussein's sons] Uday and Qusay," says Don North, a senior TV adviser to the IMN.

Those problems led to more problems. Ahmad al-Rikabi, a former London bureau chief of Radio Free Iraq, quit as head of IMN TV and returned to London because he thought the IMN was allotted inadequate resources and was losing to Iranian television the battle for the hearts and minds of Iraqis. In July [2003], IMN staff went on strike to protest working for 35 days without pay. North, on medical leave as of [October 2003] has reservations about returning because of the dodgy way the IMN has been run.[1] And when the IMN's program manager, Mike Furlong, and its government liaison, Robert Reilly, left after their initial contracts expired, they were inexplicably replaced by a man with no media experience whatsoever, John Sandrock.

The Need to Limit Anti-Americanism

But for all these practical shortcomings, bigger problems were inherent in the very nature of the undertaking. On the one hand, the American presence in Iraq was intended to nurture basic democratic liberties. On the other, as an occupying power, the Americans needed to root out the Baathist regime[2] and eradicate support for its values. For the IMN,

---

1. North did not return to the IMN.   2. The Baath Party was the former ruling political party of Iraq, headed by Saddam Hussein.

that meant serving as a model for a free press while at the same time ensuring that anti-American and pro-Baathist sentiments did not flourish on air. And it's between that rock and hard place that the Coalition Provisional Authority (CPA), the American-orchestrated transitional body running postwar Iraq, ran into trouble.

As criticism of his authority appeared in Iraqi media, occupying authority chief L. Paul Bremer III placed controls on IMN content and clamped down on the independent media in Iraq, closing down some Iraqi-run newspapers and radio and television stations. Those actions led to charges by Iraqis and external observers that the Americans were touting liberty but ruling by tyranny. "You have this dynamic of nonexistent planning, no clear goals, uncertain allocation plans and failure," says Anthony Borden, executive director of the Institute on War and Peace Reporting, about the entire media undertaking. Under the best of circumstances, managing the media in a newly destabilized Iraq would have been a tricky balancing act. But as a result of mismanagement and general confusion on the part of the Bush administration about the nature of American power in Iraq, the job has become harder than it needed to be.

Iraqi Journalism Becomes "a Farce"

The contradiction between encouraging democratic values and ruling by force was built into the IMN's very origins. Early this year [2003], the Pentagon hired not a media outlet but a San Diego–based defense contractor, the Scientific Applications International Corp. (SAIC), to develop a multimedia operation in postwar Iraq. Although this new outfit was intended to become a kind of public broadcasting system, the SAIC's orientation was more toward information control: One of SAIC's specializations, for example, is "Information Dominance/Command and Control." The IMN was created in April [2003], and it wasn't long before journalists hired by the SAIC realized their double role: The occupying authority told them to stop conducting man-on-the-street interviews because some were too critical of the American presence, and to stop including readings of the *Koran* as part of cultural programming. In the middle of the summer, against North's objections, the Americans forced IMN TV to run an hour-long program on recently issued occupying authority laws. The program was produced by the CPA-run interim justice ministry without journalists' participation and repeated much of the information presented in another hour-long segment on the subject that had been hosted by al-Rikabi. "It was an interest group massaging [itself] without a journalist being a host," says North. "A lot of Iraqis I know saw what a farce it was. That was the sort of thing that was degrading the quality of journalism at IMN and making it less credible."

Destroying Media Credibility in Iraq

[The Iraq Media Network] seemed to go off the rails after a few months. . . . It became a conduit for information from CPA [Coalition Provisional Authority], from Ambassador [Paul] Bremer. I have no problem with CPA explaining themselves to the Iraqi people. In fact, I'm an advocate for this. It's very necessary. But not to the detriment of a station that was formed for the Iraqis. Credibility with a radio or TV station is a very fragile commodity, and unfortunately after two or three months, they had destroyed this credibility that I think we started out with.

Don North, National Public Radio, October 17, 2003.

The IMN has also said that it wants to take over the offices of the independent television broadcasting station in Mosul.[3] In early May [2003], the Pentagon wanted to seize the station for including Al-Jazeera in its broadcast. The officer in charge refused to carry out the order because she didn't want to intimidate the station's journalists. Now the American authority wants direct control over the facilities so it can have a broadcasting foothold in northern Iraq, despite the fact that the station has aired more hours of IMN programming than the occupying authority demands. But it also wants to be able to run its own programs, all of which conform to the authority's content guidelines. "Rough but perfectly serviceable Iraqi stations are being swallowed up or chased off air by IMN," wrote Rohan Jayasekera for *Index on Censorship*, an in-

3. This attempt was unsuccessful.

ternational media-watchdog group. Jayasekera, who visited Iraq in late spring [2003], adds, "Iraqi broadcasters outside the IMN loop are scathing about IMN's own broadcast record, but appear powerless to stop the IMN from having its way." It's no wonder that Iraqis have seen the IMN as more of a propaganda outlet than a news station, and turned to stations like Al-Jazeera and Iran's Al-Alam.

Much of this is the result of the American authority's confusion over the IMN's purpose: Can it be both the occupiers' mouthpiece and a PBS-style network at the same time? Even Furlong, who was program manager for the first three months and generally supports U.S. efforts in Iraq, admits there is a conceptual problem. "Both roles can't be done by the same animal," he says. John Langlois, senior media adviser for USAID's [U.S. Agency for International Development's] Office of Transition Initiatives, agrees, saying, "IMN or any other entity that must act as a voice for a governing authority is always going to have difficulty coming across as an objective public broadcaster."

The Iraqis aren't waiting for the Americans to figure all this out. Many private media have already developed since Hussein's downfall. At the same time, some of these have proven decidedly hostile to their purported liberators: In July [2003], for example, the Shia newspaper *Al-Mustaqila* ran an article headlined "Death to all spies and those who cooperate with the U.S.; killing them is a religious duty."

Caution Has Led to Censorship

How should the Americans respond to such threats? Bremer's team has erred on the side of caution rather than liberty. In June [2003], Bremer issued a nine-point list of "prohibited activity" that included incitement to violence, support for the Baath Party, and publishing material that is patently false and calculated to promote opposition to the occupying authority. According to the *Index on Censorship*, Maj. Gen. David Petraeus admitted to reporters in Iraq that "what we are looking at is censorship, but you can censor something that is intended to inflame passions." Under these rules, *Al-Mustaqila*, after running its anti-American article, was closed down.

But according to a number of observers inside and outside Iraq, other cases have not been so clear cut, the appeals process has been practically nonexistent and the CPA rules are written so broadly that they could ban almost any criticism of the American authority. This summer [2003], an Iraqi newspaper in Najaf and radio station in Baghdad were closed, though the administration reveals few details about why. In another case, an Iraqi newspaper published an article comparing Bremer to Hussein—but anonymously, for fear it would be interpreted as an incitement. "I suspect that they often don't understand how journalism works," says North about the occupying authority. Indeed, Bremer issued his rules in part as a response to a false story about soldiers raping two Iraqi girls, even though the newspaper that ran the story fired the responsible reporters when the error was discovered. It would be better, advises North, to meet speech with counter-speech rather than the censor's gavel. Not to mention that closing down media outlets may do more to inflame passions than letting them publish amid the sea of independent outfits.

The occupying authority has taken some of these criticisms to heart. It is now developing an independent media commission, run by journalists rather than the U.S. Army, to enforce Bremer's rules more judiciously and to develop a more rational set of media regulations. Still, the commission will have its limits. That's because the real problem isn't that the Iraqis don't understand the need for media regulation; it's that the regulations are not a product of the will and interest of the Iraqis themselves. And that's a problem that's likely to endure as long as the Americans are the ones doing the regulating. According to the *Index on Censorship*, Bremer, reflecting on the new freedoms in Iraq, told journalists in June [2003] there that they were no longer constrained by the government and were now "free to criticize whoever, or whatever, you want."

Except, of course, the liberators themselves.

"Working on limited resources and a tattered infrastructure, the sprouting of [free] media outlets virtually overnight [in Iraq] is remarkable."

The U.S. Occupation of Iraq Has Resulted in Iraqi Media Freedom

Ilene R. Prusher

The U.S. occupation of Iraq has stimulated the proliferation of free media expression in Iraq, according to Ilene R. Prusher in the following viewpoint. Under former Iraqi president Saddam Hussein, Iraqi media was strictly controlled, but now Iraqis have a wide variety of media to choose from, maintains Prusher. She notes that Iraqis are enthusiastically embracing their new freedom of expression. Prusher is a staff writer for the *Christian Science Monitor*, a daily international newspaper.

As you read, consider the following questions:
1. What are some examples of the way free media is increasing in Iraq, as cited by the author?
2. How did Saddam Hussein use the media, according to Prusher?
3. What is the next step in the development of Iraqi media freedom, as cited by Omar Ghareb?

Seven years ago [in 1996], a customer walked into Falah Abdulrahman Mohamad Salih's television store and insisted on a barter: One of your televisions for one of my satellite dishes.

Under [former Iraqi president] Saddam Hussein, who kept an almost Orwellian[1] lid on information, satellite dishes were banned. So Mr. Salih tried to hide the round, white saucer inside some laundry lines. A few days later at 4 A.M., security police came to his door and, with his wife and children crying, hauled him off to prison.

The six grueling months there in 1996 makes these days all the sweeter. Salih was the first shopkeeper in Kirkuk [Iraq] to line up the large white dishes in front of his store, less than 48 hours after the Iraqi dictator's regime withered away. Now at least five stores offering satellite dishes have sprouted around the shopping district, selling 400 to 500 channels for about $350. That's a pricy sum, but in a country craving a window on the outside world, Salih's satellites are selling, quite literally, like hotcakes.

"Now I am a free man," says Salih in halting English. "How could we have lived under this regime?"

New Media Outlets Proliferating

In the two weeks since Kirkuk fell to a mix of Kurdish and US forces [in April 2003], free media outlets have been busting out all over: An Internet cafe opened its doors; a radio station called the Voice of Kirkuk started broadcasting part time; a newspaper called *New Kurdistan*, published in the autonomous northern city of Sulaymaniyah, started circulating here; and people are tuning into several Kurdish television channels broadcasting from the self-rule zone, an offense which in the past could have landed a person in jail, at best.

The race to let new voices be heard is also on in Baghdad, where a new newspaper began its first run [in April 2003]. The offices of what was the state-run *Al-Iraq* newspaper are being used to put out a new daily called *Al-Ittihad*, meaning unity. But that paper—as well as the radio, television, and

---

1. state-enforced conformity through indoctrination and fear; based on George Orwell's novel *1984*

newspaper outlets here in Kirkuk—are all being sponsored by one Kurdish political party, the PUK [Patriotic Union of Kurdistan], which has been spreading its resources from its quasi-capital in Sulaymaniyah to other parts of Iraq.

The development of a culture that appreciates free speech and press freedoms may not germinate overnight. Still, working on limited resources and a tattered infrastructure, the sprouting of media outlets virtually overnight is remarkable. And in many parts of the world, Europe included, it is not unusual for major newspapers to be affiliated with political parties.

Omar Ghareb, the head of the media department for Kirkuk, a city under the de facto civilian control of the PUK, says others will be free to set up shop, too.

"If we have more outlets that are independent, it would be better, in order to represent all peoples, not just one party," says Ghareb, who is also a journalist. "I'm sure that freedom is here to stay in Kirkuk, and lots of papers will be published, because people here are more cultured than you would think."

Suppression Under Hussein

There were once three major newspapers published here in Kurdish, according to Ghareb, but all of them closed down after Mr. Hussein's branch of the Baath [political] Party rose to power in 1968. Papers in the Turkmen language were also forbidden, and the only publication available here, besides government propaganda published in Baghdad, was a weekly used for "Arabization purposes," Ghareb says, a reference to the Baath Party's policy of moving Arabs from southern Iraq into what was a primarily Kurdish city.

"The paper would show that this city was only an Arabic city. It boasted how the government was doing good services for the people in Kirkuk and how everything was going well," says Ghareb. "They did it so people would get an inaccurate picture."

All of Iraq's neighbors live with varying degrees of media restrictions, while some, such as Syria and Saudi Arabia, treat mass media primarily as an organ for relaying the government's version of events. But Hussein heightened media control to almost farcical levels.

Last year [2002], the US-based Freedom House organization noted Iraq as a front-runner among the world's most repressive regimes. Hussein's oldest son, Uday, served as head of the Iraqi Journalist's Union and owned 11 newspapers, as well as television and radio stations. The papers always ran pictures of his father on the front cover, sometimes the same one day after day. Insulting the president or senior government officials was legally punishable by death.

Signs of Freedom in Iraq

• The Baghdad symphony is performing, and their concerts are also being televised. The conductor of the symphony said, "We're trying to show the world that Iraqis have a great culture."—Hisham Sharaf, at a performance of the Baghdad Symphony, June 12, 2003. . . .

• 150 newspapers on the streets of Baghdad help get out the news of a free Iraq. Ali Jabar is quoted as saying, "Every day I buy a different paper. I like them all." Says a newspaper editor: "We can't train staff fast enough. People are desperate here for a neutral free press after 30 years of a totalitarian state."—Saad al-Bazzaz, editor of the *Azzaman Daily* in Baghdad, July 8, 2003.

• Satellite dishes are the most popular items for sale in Baghdad. "I want to watch all of the world, all channels in the world. I want to watch freedom."—Mohammed al-Khayat, an Iraqi who just purchased his first satellite dish, April 26, 2003.

"100 Days of Progress in Iraq," www.whitehouse.gov.

Now, in a country accustomed to seeing the media as a tool of regime control, an Iraq under a US-sponsored rebuilding program will have to contend with encouraging press freedoms as part of the larger "de-Baathification" process.

"It is hoped that there will be much more freedom of expression in Iraq now, and there will be a more free press emerging," says Khaled Chibane, a member of the Middle East department of Amnesty International in London. "But until there is an official authority in place, there is a power vacuum, and people are mainly expressing themselves in the street. Once things settle and some sort of authority begins to appear, people will start to address the issues of press freedom."

Enthusiasm About New Freedoms

Not only Kurds are enthusiastic about the unshackling of information access in the regime's wake.

Two ethnic Turkmens—whose language is an offshoot of Turkish—are checking out new satellite dishes on the steps of Salih's store. They say they've already bought one and are enjoying watching television stations from Turkey. "If we turned on the television in the past, the only news was what Saddam did today," says Sabah Nur eh-Din. "We had only two channels. It would have been better to turn the television off and just paste up a picture of Saddam on the screen."

His friend, Abbas Ali, concurs. "We used to go to sleep at 10 P.M. Now we stay up until 4 or 5 A.M. because we can't get enough." Still desperate for war news, they tune to CNN, BBC [British Broadcasting Corporation], and what appears to be a local favorite, Fox. They like it, people here say, because it has been the most supportive of the war.

For many here, the only foreign channels they can understand are in Arabic, and they are deeply resentful of the most prominent one, Qatar-based Al-Jazeera.

Abu Bakr Mohammed Amin, an elderly man in red-checkered headdress visiting Salih's television shop, gives them a dismissive flick of the wrist: "They only knew how to support Saddam," he says.

Periodical Bibliography

The following articles have been selected to supplement the diverse views presented in this chapter.

Joel Beinin — "An Obligation to Question Prevailing Wisdom," *Nation*, December 30, 2001.

Patrisia Gonzales and Roberto Rodriquez — "Censoring Our Way to Freedom," *Progressive Populist*, June 1, 2003.

Adam Groves — "September 11: A Great Day for Censors," *Gauntlet*, May 2002.

Greg Hitt — "Bush Aims to Mute Religious Critics of Attack on Iraq," *Wall Street Journal*, February 13, 2003.

Charles L. Klotzer — "Censorship: A Two-Front War," *St. Louis Journalism Review*, April 2003.

Leonard Kniffel — "Who Wants to Be the First to Go to Jail?" *American Libraries*, August 2002.

John Leo — "'Free Speech Zones' Squelch Right to Disagree," *Conservative Chronicle*, May 14, 2003.

Charles Levendosky — "President Bush: Make Those Protestors Disappear," *Humanist*, January/February 2004.

Marvin Olasky — "Fanatical Muslim Violence Undermining Press Freedom," *Human Events*, December 16, 2002.

Bill O'Reilly — "Dissent Stinks If It Exploits the Pain of GIs," *Los Angeles Times*, May 4, 2004.

Sara Paretsky — "The New Censorship: Sara Paretsky on the Chilling Climate in America, Where a Visit to a Foreign-Language Website Can Get You Arrested, and the FBI Can Search Library Records for Dissenting Books," *New Statesman*, June 2, 2003.

Stephen B. Presser — "What Would Jefferson Do?" *Chronicles*, August 2003.

Kevin V. Ryan — "Patriot Act Is Right and Just," *Human Events*, September 15, 2003.

Joel Simon — "Look Who's Inspiring Global Censorship," *Columbia Journalism Review*, January/February 2002.

CHAPTER 4

Is Freedom in the United States Threatened by Censorship?

Chapter Preface

The majority of people in the United States greatly value freedom. In fact, to most Americans, freedom is what distinguishes their country from many others. Following the September 11, 2001, terrorist attacks, President George W. Bush voiced this feeling when he said: "Why do [the terrorists] hate us? . . . They hate our freedoms—our freedom of religion, our freedom of speech, our freedom to vote and assemble and disagree with each other." However, while most Americans believe in the importance of protecting their freedom, they greatly disagree on the extent to which censorship is harmful to it. As a result, there is a significant divide in public opinion over how much censorship should occur in the United States. Some Americans believe censorship is necessary, while others are adamantly opposed to it.

This fact is revealed in a 2003 report by the First Amendment Center, an organization that works to preserve and protect freedom of expression. The report, "State of the First Amendment," examines American attitudes toward censorship and shows that while the majority of respondents agree that Americans enjoy great freedom, they do not agree on the best way to maintain that freedom. A large number of participants in the study disapproved of censorship, but there were also a large number who advocated it. For example, only 60 percent of those surveyed said that the press should be allowed to freely criticize the U.S. military. Forty-six percent said the press has too much freedom in the United States and should be more strictly censored. Attitudes of the survey participants toward offensive speech were also split, with a large number of those surveyed advocating some censorship. Less than half the respondents believed that people should be allowed to say things in public that might be offensive to religious groups, and only 38 percent said they supported the right to say things that might offend racial groups. Fifty-five percent opposed the right of people to publicly display art that might be offensive to others.

As "State of the First Amendment" shows, the impact of censorship on freedom is a controversial topic. While many

Americans are opposed to censorship, many others believe that censorship is necessary in society and not a threat to freedom. The authors in the following chapter examine some of the ways this battle has been waged in U.S. society and offer different opinions on how censorship and freedom should coexist in the United States.

> "*When government acts to restrict what our children can see or hear, those restrictions bind the rest of us as well, including the millions of Americans who have no children at all.*"

Government Regulation of Broadcasters Is a Threat to Freedom

Adam Thierer

The government should not censor broadcast media, maintains Adam Thierer in the following viewpoint. By restricting media to protect children, the government is also unnecessarily and unconstitutionally censoring what millions of adults are exposed to, Thierer points out. He argues that parents should be the ones to impose censorship on children, not the federal government. Thierer is director of telecommunications studies at the Cato Institute, a nonprofit public policy research institute.

As you read, consider the following questions:
1. Why is censorship on an individual/parental level different from government censorship, according to Thierer?
2. Why are some television shows altering their content, according to the author?
3. In Thierer's opinion, what are policy makers really doing in the name of "protecting the children"?

L ike millions of other Americans, I will be glued to my television set on Sunday night [in June 2004] watching the season finale of HBO's critically acclaimed series *The Sopranos* to see who "gets it," or even just to hear Tony or one of his mobster buddies say "Forgetaboutit!" one last time this season.

But one person who definitely won't be watching *The Sopranos* finale on Sunday night is my young daughter. The violence, profanity, and sexual content are not something I want her exposed to. I'm not sure what the right age is for children to see such programming, but at the point my wife and I think she's ready, we'll talk to her about such shows before we sit down to watch them with her.

While all parents face this same dilemma of figuring out what to let their children watch, the choice my wife and I make for our child may not be the same choice the couple across the street makes for their kids. But that's the nature of life in a free society. It's filled with tough choices, especially when it comes to raising kids.

Government Censorship Is Unwanted

There is another alternative, of course. Our government could decide for us which shows are best for our children, or perhaps just determine which hours of the day certain shows could be aired in an attempt to shield our children's eyes and ears from them. While there are some who would welcome such a move, I would hope that there are still some other parents like me out there who aren't comfortable with the idea of calling in Uncle Sam to play the role of surrogate parent. When government acts to restrict what our children can see or hear, those restrictions bind the rest of us as well, including the millions of Americans who have no children at all.

Even if lawmakers have the best interests of children in mind, I take great offense at the notion that government officials must do this job for me and every other American family. Censorship on an individual/parental level is a fundamental part of being a good parent. But censorship at a governmental level is an entirely different matter because it means a small handful of individuals get to decide what the whole nation is permitted to see, hear or think.

Danger of Raising Indecency Fines

The Broadcast Decency Enforcement Act of 2004 . . . would dramatically increase fines for obscene, indecent, or profane broadcasts, sending a widening chill into the atmosphere of free expression protected by the First Amendment [the act had not passed as of this writing].

The heart of our objection to the bill is that it relies upon the FCC's [Federal Communications Commission's] definition of "indecency" which is already vague. Because of the vagueness, speakers must engage in speech at their peril, guessing what the FCC will determine to be prohibited. Increasing fines merely exacerbates the problem, particularly for small broadcasters. Rather than face a potentially ruinous fine, smaller broadcasters are more likely to remain silent.

Guessing incorrectly can have important ramifications for a broadcaster, including huge fines and possibly loss of its broadcasting license. Vague laws and interpretations create traps for broadcasters because they are unsure what conduct or speech will constitute indecency. Rather than have broadcasters act at their peril, the law prefers reasonable notice of what conduct will give rise to legal consequences, so that the speaker may act accordingly. Vagueness results in chilling of communications that may well NOT be indecent or profane, simply because the cost to the broadcaster of being wrong is too great. Vagueness encourages silence instead of robust debate. "Uncertain meanings inevitably lead citizens to 'steer far wider of the unlawful zone' . . . than if the boundaries of the forbidden areas were clearly marked." The bottom line is that broadcasters enjoy First Amendment protection. The uncertainty inherent in the definition (or lack thereof) of "indecency" will inevitably lead broadcasters to avoid certain speech because that speech may later be deemed indecent, and the broadcaster faces tremendous liability because of the increase in the fines.

American Civil Liberties Union, February 10, 2004.

OK, OK . . . enough of the heated rhetoric, you say. This guy is just huffin'-and-puffin' about some Orwellian[1] scenario that doesn't exist in this country and never could. After all, nobody's seriously talking about censoring *The Sopranos* or anything else on cable TV, right? They're just talking

---

1. In George Orwell's novel *1984*, the government controlled the people's access to all information.

about the censoring broadcasters, who really don't get that much heat from regulators anyway, correct?

The Threat of Increased Censorship

Wrong on both counts. Building on the momentum of the new indecency witch hunt that is driving many talk shows hosts off broadcast radio, and has television shows like *E.R.* altering their content to keep censors happy, lawmakers are now putting cable and satellite programming in their crosshairs. There are discussions taking place in Congress today [2004] about "codes of conduct" for cable TV, and even a government-approved "family-friendly" tier on cable systems. Joe Barton (R-Tex.), chairman of the House Commerce Committee, which oversees media industry regulation, recently told a crowd of cable industry officials that censorship of pay TV is "an issue whose time is coming. I think we're approaching the time when whatever we apply to the broadcasters, in some way, voluntarily or involuntarily, is going to be applied to cable."

Step back for a moment and think about what this means for popular cable programs such as [television networks] FX's *The Shield*, Comedy Central's *South Park* or *The Daily Show*, Showtime's *Queer as Folk* or *The L Word*, or any of the amazing programs that air Sundays on HBO in addition to *The Sopranos* (*Sex and the City, Curb Your Enthusiasm, Six Feet Under,* and *Deadwood*). Are we worse off for having these shows in this world? Some policymakers apparently think so and have—in the name of "protecting the children"—put the creative community on notice that they no longer have the artistic freedom to make such programs on their own terms. And Americans who have grown to love such shows will be forced to live with sanitized versions of these programs. (Would a bleeped, "kiddie-approved" version of *The Sopranos* even be worth watching?)

Parents need to stand up and tell the government to stay out of their business and then get down to the serious business of educating their children about the realities of this world, including what we see and hear in the media today. Government censorship is never a good solution in a free society. As Tony Soprano would say, "Forgetaboutit!"

"There is nearly universal concern about the state of our public airwaves. . . . The public is outraged by the increasingly crude content they see and hear in their media today."

Government Regulation of Broadcasters Is Necessary

Jonathan S. Adelstein

Broadcast content has become increasingly offensive to Americans and harmful to children, asserts Jonathan S. Adelstein in the following viewpoint. He contends that complaints against broadcast media content have risen dramatically and interprets this as a sign that Americans have a strong desire to stop the broadcasting of crude content. He believes that government regulation of inappropriate content should be more strict, and that broadcasters share the responsibility of enforcing censorship of inappropriate material. Adelstein is commissioner of the Federal Communications Commission.

As you read, consider the following questions:
1. While parents can block cable television programs they consider inappropriate, why is this not enough to protect children from inappropriate broadcast material, according to the author?
2. What is the cornerstone of the broadcaster's social compact with the public, as cited by Adelstein?
3. How do culture and media influence each other, in the author's opinion?

Jonathan S. Adelstein, address before the U.S. Senate Committee on Commerce, Science, and Transportation, Washington, DC, February 11, 2004.

L ike many of you, I sat down with my wife and children to watch the Super Bowl [in 2004]. I was expecting a showcase of America's best talent, both on and off the field, and the apotheosis of our cultural creativity during the entertainment and advertising portions. Instead, like millions of others, I was appalled by the halftime show—not just for the shock-value stunt at the end [when performer Janet Jackson's bare breast was revealed], but for the overall raunchy performance displayed in front of so many children—one in five American children were watching, according to reports. And the advertising set a new low for what should air during family time.

The Super Bowl is a rare occasion for families to get together to enjoy a national pastime everyone should be able to appreciate. Instead, a special family occasion was truly disrespected.

Inappropriate Content During the Super Bowl

I could highlight any number of tasteless commercials that depicted sexual and bodily functions in a vile manner. Any sense of internal controls appeared out the window, so long as the advertiser paid the multi-million dollar rate.

One commercial that really stung my family, and many other parents with whom I spoke, was a violent trailer for an unrated horror movie. It showed horrible monsters with huge fangs attacking people. I literally jumped out of my chair to get between the TV and my three-year old. Other parents told me they couldn't reach for the remote control fast enough. I wonder how those who chose to broadcast such violence can sleep at night when they gave so many American children nightmares.

No parent should have to jump in front of the TV to block their children from such images, whether during a commercial or a halftime show. No parent should feel guilty for not being with their child every single moment in case they need to block the TV during what most would consider to be a family viewing event.

The entire Super Bowl broadcast was punctuated by inappropriate images that were an embarrassment for our country. The halftime show, with its global appeal, was a wasted opportunity to showcase the best that U.S. culture has to offer. The U.S. has the world's greatest musical culture to promote across the globe, and that includes the many artists who performed at the event. Our musicians and artists offer a vibrant musical melting pot that expands our horizons and enriches our culture. As a musician myself, I am proud of artists who every day express their creativity without trying to one up each other in shock value. There is plenty of magnificent talent here for the whole family to enjoy. It is those performances that broadcasters should showcase. Instead, the halftime show needlessly descended into lewdness and crassness.

Increasingly Crude Content

This latest incident is only the tip of the iceberg. There is nearly universal concern about the state of our public airwaves. I personally received more than 10,000 emails last week [February 2004] and the FCC [Federal Communications Commission] received more than 200,000. But that pales in comparison to the number of people who over the past year expressed their outrage to me about the homogenization and crassness of the media. The public is outraged by the increasingly crude content they see and hear in their media today. They are fed up with the sex, violence, and profanity flooding into our homes. . . .

Complaints are exploding that our airwaves are increasingly dominated by graphic and shocking entertainment. Some observe that broadcasters are only responding to competition from cable programming. Take MTV, a cable network known for pushing the envelope. It's owned by Viacom, which also owns CBS. It's no coincidence that MTV produced the halftime show. But the network thoughtlessly applied the cable programmer's standards during the Super Bowl—the ultimate family event.

As a musician, I recognize that channels like MTV have a place in our society. I also understand and respect that many would prefer that they not intrude into the mainstream of American family life. Parents who purchase cable television have the legal right to block any channel they don't consider appropriate for their children. More parents should be made aware of this right. Free over-the-air broadcasting, however, offers no such alternative to parents. For broadcast material designed for mature audiences, it's a matter of the right time and place.

Need for Stricter Standards

Enough is enough. As a parent and an FCC Commissioner, I share the public's disgust with increasingly crude radio and television content.

I've only served on the Commission for about a year, but I'm proud that we've stepped up our enforcement in that time. And we need to ramp it up even further. In my view, gratuitous use of swear words or nudity have no place in broadcasting.

Gamble. © 1990 by *The Florida Times-Union*: King Features Syndicate. Reproduced by permission of King Features Syndicate.

We need to act forcefully now. Not surprisingly, complaints before the FCC are rising rapidly, with more than 240,000 complaints covering 370 programs last year [2003]. In the cases on which I have voted, I have supported going to the statutory maximum for fines. But even this statutory maximum—$27,500 per incident—is woefully inadequate. I welcome the efforts by Congress to authorize us to increase fines substantially across all our areas of jurisdiction.

Awaiting such authority, I've pushed for new approaches to deter indecency. We can increase the total amount of fines by fining for each separate utterance within the same program segment. And we need to hold hearings to consider revoking broadcasters' licenses in serious, repeated cases. I worked last April [2003] to have the FCC put broadcasters on notice that we were taking these steps to establish a stronger enforcement regime. Our challenge now is to act more quickly when we get complaints, and to ensure that our complaint procedures are as consumer-friendly as possible.

But there are limits to what the FCC can do. We must balance strict enforcement of the indecency laws with the First Amendment. If we overstep, we risk losing the narrow constitutional authority we now have to enforce the rules. Nevertheless, many cases I have seen in my tenure are so far past any boundary of decency that any broadcaster should have known the material would violate our rules.

Responsibility of Broadcasters

So it may very well take more than the FCC to turn this around. We are not the only ones with a public trust to keep the airwaves free from obscene, indecent and profane material. Broadcasters are given exclusive rights to use the public airwaves in the public interest. The broadcasters themselves bear much of the responsibility to keep our airwaves decent. As stewards of the airwaves, broadcasters are in the position to step up and use their public airwaves in a manner that celebrates our country's tremendous cultural heritage. Or they can continue down the path of debasing that heritage. Their choices ultimately will guide our enforcement.

Serving local communities is the cornerstone of the broadcaster's social compact with the public. When people choose to become licensed broadcasters, they understand that a public service responsibility comes with that privilege. In his famous remarks lamenting the "vast wasteland" of television, [former FCC chairman] Newton Minow rightly observed that, "an investment in broadcasting is buying a share in public responsibility." Every broadcaster should take that to heart. Public responsibility may mean passing up an opportunity to pander to the nation's whims and current ratings trends when it is more important to stand up and meet the needs of the local community.

Broadcasters need to show more corporate responsibility. They must rise above commercial pressures, and recognize the broader social problems they may be compounding.

Protecting American Culture

Many factors set the cultural and moral tone of our society. I welcome the attention that our indecency enforcement is receiving. I don't think of it as silly or overblown, as some have suggested. The question before America is whether the coarsening of our media is responsible for the coarsening of our culture, or vice versa. My answer is both. They feed on each other.

Media consolidation only intensifies the pressures. Fast-growing conglomerates focus on the bottom line above all else. The FCC should reconsider its dramatic weakening of media ownership limits last summer [2003].

Local broadcasters also need the ability to reject network programming that doesn't meet their communities' standards. The FCC must preserve the critical back-and-forth local affiliates have with the networks in the fight against indecency. . . .

During the Super Bowl, and on far too many other occasions, people feel assaulted by what is broadcast at them. My job is to protect our families from the broadcast of obscene, indecent or profane material. That also means promoting healthy fare for our children. After all, the airwaves are owned by the American people, and the public is eager to take some control back.

"Media ownership rules are essential to a healthy democracy because they prevent any one owner from dominating any particular media market."

Censorship by Media Conglomerates Threatens Democracy

Gene Kimmelman

The Federal Communications Commission (FCC) regulates mass media in the United States. In 2003 the commission made changes to the rules governing media ownership, including the relaxation of a number of restrictions on the ownership of radio and television. The following viewpoint is excerpted from the congressional testimony of Gene Kimmelman prior to those changes. Kimmelman argues that ownership rules should not be relaxed because diversity of media is an essential part of democracy. By easing ownership rules, contends Kimmelman, the FCC will exacerbate a harmful trend in which media in the United States is dominated by a small number of corporations. Kimmelman is an expert on deregulation and consumer protection issues.

As you read, consider the following questions:
1. How did the U.S. Supreme Court interpret the First Amendment protection of the press in *Associated Press v. United States*, as cited by the author?
2. What form of news media is a key input for all other media, as reported by Kimmelman?

Gene Kimmelman, testimony before the U.S. Senate Committee on Commerce, Science, and Transportation, Washington, DC, May 13, 2003.

"Independent, aggressive journalism strengthens American democracy, improves the lives of its citizens, checks the abuses of powerful people, supports the weakest members of society, connects us all to one another, educates and entertains us. News matters."

"Broadly speaking, three factors distinguish newspapers from one another: ambitions, resources and values. Ownership is probably the greatest influence on all three."

—Leonard Downie Jr. and Walter Kaiser

It does not follow that just because the world has changed, ownership limits must be removed or significantly relaxed. Such action is not supported by a careful analysis of exactly how the media landscape has changed:

Increasing Media Consolidation

• Yes, the Internet exploded onto the media scene, but no, it is not a significant source of news and information for most consumers. In fact, for the few who rely upon the Internet as a source of news, the major sites consumers visit are owned by large media companies.

• Yes, cable has steadily grown to challenge the broadcast networks, but no, cable does not provide any meaningful local news and information other than by retransmitting local TV broadcast stations. In the few cases where there is a local cable news channel, it is often owned by a local broadcaster.

• Yes, there are many more local TV stations than 25 years ago [1978], but only about half of local channels provide local news coverage. . . .

• Yes, on the national level there are many more news and entertainment channels than 25 years ago, but no, this does not translate into very much diversity of ownership. National broadcast networks and one cable company (AOL, Time Warner) own all of these news channels. These same five companies control most of the leading primetime entertainment programs. And they get much more of their primetime programming from in-house studios than 25 years ago, reducing competitive sources of popular programming.

While it appears that a majority of the FCC's [Federal Communications Commission's] Commissioners continue to believe that media ownership rules must be changed, the facts strongly point in the opposite direction. The FCC, in its rulemaking proceedings, has compiled data that massive consolidation of ownership and control of media—during a period of an explosion of outlets—has left virtually all TV broadcasting and newspaper markets so concentrated that further mergers would undermine competition. And the FCC has an enormous factual record, loaded with both quantitative and qualitative evidence, demonstrating very few changes in the sources consumers rely upon for their most important local news and information. . . .

If the FCC relaxes media ownership rules because it no longer believes it must attempt to follow the Supreme Court's interpretation of our Constitution's First Amendment—promoting "the widest possible dissemination of information from diverse and antagonistic sources," the Commission will be underestimating the importance of diverse local and national media ownership to the detriment of our democracy.

Media Is Critical for Democracy

Why does this matter? Because the major media—television and newspaper—play a critical role in gathering and disseminating the information that citizens rely upon to make the judgments and decisions that define our democracy. It matters because the media ownership rules ensure that there are multiple media owners and diverse media viewpoints in every community. They prevent one company from having too much control over media content in any one place at any one time. The rules provide checks and balances that help media companies not only serve as watchdogs for government and business, but also for each other.

Weakening the nation's media ownership rules is likely to spark an avalanche of mergers that would reduce competition and diversity of ownership. Not only would this harm social and political discussion in a community, but it could raise the costs of advertising in local media—costs which are passed on to consumers.

Media ownership rules are essential to a healthy democracy because they prevent any one owner from dominating any particular media market. Americans depend on mass media to learn about current affairs, keep abreast of local issues, and make informed political choices. These rules were adopted to ensure that the public would receive a wide range of contrasting perspectives from the media, not simply the opinion of a dominant media owner in a particular community. . . .

The largest media giants are now trying to get rid of media ownership limits, claiming they infringe on corporate "free speech." Even [FCC] Chairman [Michael] Powell has asserted that the First Amendment is simply a tool to protect citizens from government intrusion on speech, not from corporate limitations on speech. But Powell's view is totally inconsistent with Supreme Court precedent confirming the government's power and need to limit both corporate and governmental excess in order to preserve the public's marketplace of ideas.

The Supreme Court articulated the fundamental meaning of the First Amendment in *Associated Press v. United States:*

> The First Amendment . . . rests on the assumption that the widest possible dissemination of information from diverse and antagonistic sources is essential to the welfare of the public, that a free press is a condition of a free society. Surely a command that the government itself shall not impede the free flow of ideas does not afford non-governmental combinations a refuge if they impose restraints upon that constitutionally guaranteed freedom. Freedom to publish means freedom for all and not for some. Freedom to publish is guaranteed by the Constitution, but freedom to combine to keep others from publishing is not. Freedom of the press from governmental interference under the First Amendment does not sanction repression of that freedom by private interests.

Under this dynamic principle, media ownership rules should be a tool for expanding, not providing "just enough" democratic discourse. The Supreme Court has interpreted the Constitution in a manner that protects private and public activities that promote the *widest possible* dissemination of information as a fundamental element of freedom of speech. . . .

Cross-Ownership Limits Necessary

Most communities in the U.S. have one newspaper, and most communities' broadcast television markets are already either moderately or highly concentrated. When the markets for the sources of information that most Americans rely on for their news and information—newspaper and broad-cast—are already highly concentrated, taking steps that will further consolidate those markets should give us pause.

TV and Newspapers Are the Public's Most Imporant Source of All News

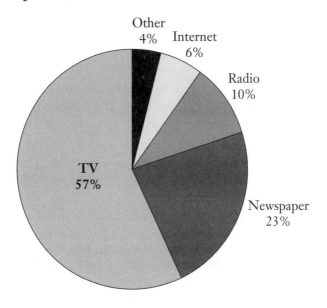

Federal Communications Commission, *Consumer Survey on Media Usage*, September 2002.

If there ever were markets that we should not allow to become even moderately concentrated, it is the markets that provide the key news and information that fuel our democracy. The FCC is sitting on a mountain of data which demonstrate that newspapers and local TV broadcast stations are precisely such markets and virtually all of them are already highly or moderately concentrated. Therefore, if the FCC changes media ownership in a manner that enables national networks to buy more local TV stations and more of those stations to combine with other TV stations in the same market, or combine with dominant newspapers in the same market, the Commission would be undermining competition within and across media and endangering democracy itself.

The majority of U.S. citizens still get their news and information from newspapers and television. On average, each newspaper has 62 reporters, each broadcast television station has 24 reporters, and each radio station has 3. And while the Internet has become a means of accessing news that some Americans use, it is simply another distribution channel, and is not a distinct means of news production. Evidence shows that the news and information available online on the Internet—especially local information—is primarily produced by the very same local newspapers and television stations that citizens turn to offline.

Furthermore, newspapers are a key input to all other media. Much of what is covered on broadcast television has its origins in newspaper stories, and television often reduces complex stories to short visual images with sound bites. [According to Leonard Downie Jr. and Walter Kaiser,]

> Television, like radio, is a relatively inefficient conveyor of factual information. The text of [Walter] Cronkite's evening news, after eliminating the commercials, would fill just over half the front page of a full-sized newspaper. A typical network evening news show now mentions from a dozen to fifteen or so different subjects, some in just a sentence, whereas a good newspaper has scores of different news items every day. A big story on television might get two minutes, or about 400 words. The *Los Angeles Times* coverage of the same big story could easily total 2,000 words.

Cable television is not a substitute for diverse, locally owned media, given that there is virtually no local cable news production. Most of the consumers who cite cable as their source for news and information, identify national, not local cable channels which offer virtually no local content: Fox News, CNN, Headline News, CNBC, and MSNBC. A number of cable systems offer one local news channel, but they are often owned by a local broadcast station, offering no new local viewpoints to the market.

Watchdog Function of the Media

Who is it that commonly uncovers the most egregious behaviors in government and the marketplace? Did corporations blow the whistle on each other to uncover crooked accounting practices [in 2002] in the midst of several of the largest bankruptcies in history? Did the regulatory agencies with oversight over these industries first get to the bottom of this corruption? Absolutely not. In many cases, it was journalists . . . that brought these problems to light. Journalists bring these problems to the government's attention and initiate the process of both public education and prompting the appropriate response to bad behavior. Legislatures, regulatory agencies and many other institutions play a significant role, but it is simply naive, and indeed impossible for them to take over the watchdog function that newspapers and television provide our society.

The media ownership rules are designed to increase the likelihood that there will be a sufficient number of independent media outlets—with strong competitive incentives between them—to provide antagonism necessary for aggressive reporting when a company involved in the media is itself engaged in this kind of practice.

Consider how last year [2002], the *Washington Post* reported questionable accounting practices by D.C.-based America Online (AOL). The investigation involved reviewing hundreds of pages of confidential AOL documents and conducting interviews with current and former AOL officials and their partners. After months of investigative work, reporter Alec Klein broke the story that AOL had indeed boosted revenues through shady advertising deals. Shortly after the *Post* published its findings, the federal government launched criminal and civil investigations, leading AOL to restate its earnings.

But what if AOL Time Warner had owned the *Post*? Investigating this kind of story is a significant investment of resources; to take a reporter off day to day work and engage in months of investigation requires a substantial financial commitment. Had AOL owned the *Post*, it seems highly unlikely that it would have invested heavily in this story when it meant not only lost staff time but also a negative effect on its bottom line.

Furthermore, this happened in a national news town, with numerous sources of investigative reporting. What would have been the outcome in a community where—like the majority of communities in America—there is only one newspaper, if that newspaper were also owned by a dominant broadcaster? . . .

Network Dominance in the Television Market

Increased concentration in the primetime television programming market illustrates the dangers to progamming competition and localism, by allowing national TV networks to grow. Despite the appearance of hundreds of different channels, the bulk of primetime offerings originate with the four national broadcast networks and AOL Time Warner. . . .

In addition, the number of independent studios in existence has dwindled dramatically since the mid-1980s. In 1985, there were 25 independent television production studios; there was little drop-off in that number between 1985 and 1992. In 2002, however, only 5 independent television studios remained. In addition, in the ten-year period between 1992 and 2002, the number of primetime television hours per week produced by network studios increased over 200%, whereas the number of primetime television hours per week produced by independent studios decreased 63%.

[According to Writers Guild of America president Victoria Ruskin] diversity of production sources has "eroded to the point of near extinction. In 1992, only 15 percent of new series were produced for a network by a company it controlled. Last year [2002], the percentage of shows produced by controlled companies more than quintupled to 77 percent. In 1992, 16 new series were produced independently of conglomerate control, last year there was one."

The ease with which broadcasters blew away the independent programmers should sound a strong cautionary alarm for Congress. . . .

The Importance of Ownership Limits

Even in the face of changed and changing media, the ownership rules are still extremely relevant. They achieve congressional goals of localism and diversity by keeping ownership decentralized, and by keeping local media entities distinct from the most dominant national players. Importantly, they underscore the Supreme Court's interpretation on our Constitution's First Amendment—promoting the widest possible dissemination of information from diverse and antagonistic sources. . . .

The cost of relaxing media ownership is very high. The cost of market failure in media markets is the price we pay when stories are *not* told, when sleazy business deals and bad accounting practices do *not* surface, when the watchdog decides that it would rather gnaw on the bone of softer news than chase down the more complicated realities that must be uncovered to make democracy function.

"*Citizens have more choice and more control over what they see, hear, or read than at any other time in history. This . . . is having a tremendous impact on our democracy.*"

Current Media Ownership Rules Promote Freedom of Speech

Michael K. Powell

In 2003 the Federal Communications Commission (FCC), which regulates mass media in the United States, made changes to the rules governing media ownership. These changes included easing a number of restrictions on ownership of radio and television. In the following viewpoint FCC chairman Michael K. Powell asserts that these changes promote competition among media networks. Powell argues that under the new rules, Americans have more programming choices than ever before. Powell has served on the FCC since 1997.

As you read, consider the following questions:
1. Compared to the 1960s is the media different today, as cited by the author?
2. According to Powell, what broadcast medium is having a profound impact on the diversity of news sources?
3. What are the advantages of localism, in the author's opinion?

Michael K. Powell, "Should the FCC Relax Its Media Ownership Rules?" *Congressional Digest*, October 2003.

Today's media marketplace is marked by abundance. Since 1966, there has been an explosion of media outlets throughout the country. Even in small towns like Burlington, Vermont, the number of voices—including cable, satellite, radio, TV stations, and newspapers—has increased over 250 percent during the last 40 years. Independent ownership of those outlets is far more diverse, with 140 percent more owners today [in 2003] than in 1960.

What does this abundance mean for the American people? It means more programming, more choice, and more control in the hands of citizens. At any given moment, our citizens have access to scores of TV networks devoted to movies, dramatic series, sports, news, and educational programming, both for adults and children; in short, niche programming to satisfy almost any of our citizens' diverse tastes.

Increasing Diversity of Media

In 1960—the "Golden Age of Television"—if you missed the half-hour evening newscast, you were out of luck. In 1980, it was no different. But today, news and public affairs programming—the fuel of our democratic society—is overflowing. There used to be three broadcast networks, each with 30 minutes of news daily. Today [in 2003], there are three 24-hour all-news networks, seven broadcast networks, and over 300 cable networks. Local networks are bringing the American public more local news than at any point in history.

The Internet is also having a profound impact on the ever-increasing desire of our citizenry to inform themselves and to do so using a wide variety of sources. Google news service brings information from 4,500 news sources to one's fingertips from around the world, all with the touch of a button. As demonstrated by this proceeding, diverse and antagonistic voices use the Internet daily to reach the American people. Whether it is the *New York Times* editorial page, or Joe Citizen using email to let his views be known to the [Federal Communications] Commission [FCC], or the use by organizations such as MoveOn.org to perform outreach to citizens, the Internet is putting the tools of democracy in the hands of speakers and listeners more and more each day.

I have not cited cable television and the Internet by accident. Their contribution to the marketplace of ideas is not linear, it is exponential. Cable and the Internet explode the model for viewpoint diversity in the media. Diversity-by-appointment has vanished. Now, the media makes itself available on our schedule, as much or as little as we want, when we want. In sum, citizens have more choice and more control over what they see, hear, or read than at any other time in history. This is a powerful paradigm shift in the American media system, and is having a tremendous impact on our democracy. . . .

The balanced set of national and local broadcast ownership rules [the FCC] adopted preserve and protect our core policy goals of diversity, competition, and localism. . . .

Protecting Viewpoint Diversity

The Commission, recognizing that "the widest possible dissemination of information from diverse and antagonistic sources is essential to the welfare of the public," introduced broadcast ownership limits that will protect viewpoint diversity. The Commission concluded that neither the newspaper-broadcast prohibition nor the TV-radio cross-ownership prohibition could be justified in larger markets in light of the abundance of diverse sources available to citizens to rely on for their news consumption.

By implementing our cross-media limits, however, the Commission will protect viewpoint diversity by ensuring that no company, or group of companies, can control an inordinate share of media outlets in a local market. We developed a Diversity Index to measure the availability of key media outlets in markets of various sizes. By breaking out markets into tiers, the Commission was able to better tailor our rules to reflect different levels of media availability in different sized markets. For the first time ever, the Commission built its data in implementing this rule directly from input received from the public on how they actually use the media to obtain news and public affairs information.

Furthermore, by instituting our local television multiple ownership rule (especially by banning mergers among the top-four stations, which the record demonstrated typically produce an independent local newscast) and our local radio ownership limit, the Commission will foster multiple independently owned media outlets in both broadcast television and radio—advancing the goal of promoting the widest dissemination of viewpoints.

Enhancing Competition

Moreover, our new broadcast ownership regulations promote competition in the media marketplace. The Commission determined that our prior local television multiple ownership limits could not be justified as necessary to promote competition because it failed to reflect the significant competition now faced by local broadcasters from cable and satellite TV services. Our revised local television limit is the first TV ownership rule to acknowledge that competition.

Modified Media Ownership Rules Summary

• A broadcast network can now own and operate local broadcast stations that reach, in total, up to 45 percent of U.S. television households. The old limit was 35 percent.

• Both newspaper-broadcast cross-ownership and television-radio cross-ownership are unrestricted in markets with nine or more television stations; allowed, subject to certain restrictions, in markets with between four and eight television stations; and prohibited in markets with three or fewer television stations.

• A company can own three television stations in markets with 18 or more television stations, and two television stations in markets with five or more television stations. But in either case, only one of the two stations can be among the top four in ratings at time of purchase.

• The number of radio stations that a company can own in a local market, which varies according to the total number of stations in the market, remains the same. But the market is now defined in terms of the Arbitron geographic market, and noncommercial stations are included in the station count.

"New Limits on Media Concentration," *Congressional Digest*, October 2003.

This new rule will enhance competition in local markets by allowing broadcast television stations to compete more effectively not only against other broadcast stations, but also against cable and/or satellite channels in that local market. In addition, the record demonstrates that these same market combinations yield efficiencies that will serve the public interest through improved or expanded services such as local news and public affairs programming and facilitating the transition to digital television through economic efficiencies.

The Commission found that our current [2003] limits on local radio ownership continue to be necessary to promote competition among local radio stations and we reaffirmed the caps set forth by Congress in the 1996 Telecommunications Act. . . . We concluded that the current method for defining radio markets was not in the public interest and thus needed to be modified. We found that the current market definition for radio markets, which relies on the signal contour of the commonly owned stations, is unsound and produces anomalous and irrational results, undermining the purpose of the rule.

We therefore adopted geographic-based market definitions, which are a more rational means for protecting competition in local markets. For example, we fixed the case of Minot, North Dakota, which under our former rules produced a market with 45 radio stations. Under our reformed market definition, Minot would have only 10 radio stations included in the relevant geographic market.

By promoting competition through the local television and radio rules, the Commission recognized that the rules may result in a number of situations where current ownership arrangements exceed ownership limits. In such cases the Commission made a limited exception to permit sales of grandfathered [previously existing] station combinations to small businesses. In so doing, the Commission sought to respect the reasonable expectations of parties that lawfully purchased groups of local radio stations that today, through redefined markets, now exceed the applicable caps. We promote competition by permitting station owners to retain any above-cap local radio clusters but not transfer them intact unless such a transfer avoids undue hardships to cluster owners that are small businesses or promote the entry into broadcasting by small businesses—many of which are minority- or female-owned.

Finally, by retaining our ban on mergers among any of the top four national broadcast networks, the Commission continues to promote competition in the national television advertising and program acquisition markets.

Fostering Localism

Recognizing that localism remains a bedrock public interest benefit, the Commission took a series of actions designed to foster localism by aligning our ownership limits with the local stations' incentives to serve the needs and interests of their local communities.

For instance, by retaining the dual network prohibition and increasing the national television ownership limit to 45 percent, the Commission promoted localism by preserving the balance of negotiating power between networks and affiliates. The national cap will allow a body of network affiliates to negotiate collectively with the broadcast networks on network programming decisions to best serve the needs of their local community, while at the same time allowing the networks to gain critical mass to prevent the flight of quality programs, such as sports and movies, to cable or satellite.

The record further demonstrated that by both raising the national cap to 45 percent and allowing for cross-ownership combinations in certain markets the Commission would promote localism. Indeed, the record showed that broadcast network owned-and-operated stations served their local communities better with respect to local news production—airing more local news programming than did affiliates. Furthermore, the record demonstrated that where newspaper-broadcast television combinations were allowed, those television stations have produced dramatically better news coverage in terms of quantity (over 50 percent more news) and quality (outpacing non-newspaper-owned television stations in news awards).

The Commission crafted a balanced set of broadcast ownership restrictions to preserve and promote the public interest goals of diversity, competition, and localism.

"I oppose this amendment [to ban flag burning] because it does not support the freedom of expression and the right to dissent."

The Proposed Flag Protection Amendment Is a Threat to Liberty in America

Gary E. May

In 2004 an amendment to the U.S. Constitution was proposed that, if passed, will ban flag desecration. In the following viewpoint, originally given as congressional testimony on May 7, 2003, Gary E. May argues that this amendment is a threat to free speech in America. He contends that while flag burning is offensive to most Americans, it is an important form of dissent essential to American democracy. A flag protection amendment would stifle that dissent, he claims. As of the writing of this viewpoint, the amendment was still being debated in Congress. May is a Vietnam veteran who lost both his legs in combat there.

As you read, consider the following questions:
1. May explains that he fought in Vietnam to support America's freedom. What would be the ultimate irony, according to him?
2. In what is the strength of the American nation founded, as argued by the author?
3. What difficult questions will a flag protection amendment raise, according to May?

Gary E. May, testimony before the U.S. House Judiciary Committee, Washington, DC, May 7, 2003.

As a Vietnam veteran who lives daily with the consequences of my service to my country, and as the son of a WWII combat veteran, and the grandson of a WWI combat veteran, I can attest to the fact that not all veterans, indeed perhaps most veterans, do not wish to exchange fought-for freedoms for protecting a tangible symbol of these freedoms. I oppose this amendment [to ban flag burning] because it does not support the freedom of expression and the right to dissent.[1]

This is among the core principles under our Constitution that my family and I served to support and defend. It would be the ultimate irony for us to place ourselves in harm's way and for my family to sacrifice to gain freedom for other nations and not to protect our freedom here at home. . . .

Fighting for Freedom

My father, Charles W. May, who died nearly a year ago [in 2002], was a WWII Army combat veteran who served in the European Theater of Operations from 1944 to 1946. He saw combat with Battery "B" 500th Armored Field Artillery Battalion, 14th Armored Division. The flag or its protection was not a powerful motivating force for himself or any of his fellow combatants. It was the fight for freedom that really mattered.

I joined the U.S. Marine Corps while still in high school in 1967. This was a time of broadening public dissent and demonstration against our involvement in Vietnam. I joined the Marines, these protests notwithstanding, because I felt that it was my duty to do so. I felt duty-bound to answer President [John F.] Kennedy's challenge to "ask not what your country can do for you; ask what you can do for your country." My country was asking for me to serve in Vietnam, ostensibly because people there were being arbitrarily denied the freedoms we enjoy as Americans.

During my service with K Company, 3rd Battalion, 27th Marines following the Tet Offensive of 1968 in Vietnam, I sustained bilateral above the knee amputations as a result of a landmine explosion on April 12, 1968. My military awards in-

1. As of the writing of this viewpoint, the amendment was still being debated in Congress.

clude the Bronze Star, with combat "V", Purple Heart, with star, Vietnam Campaign, Vietnam Service, and National Defense medals.

While serving in Vietnam, I never once heard one of my fellow Marines say they were there protecting the flag. . . .

A few years ago, near the anniversary of my injuries in Vietnam, I had a conversation with a colleague at the University [of Tennessee]. I mentioned the anniversary of my wounding to her and asked her what she was doing in 1968. Somewhat reluctantly, she said, "I was protesting the war in Vietnam." I was not offended. After all, our nation was born out of political dissent. Preservation of the freedom to dissent, even if it means using revered icons of this democracy, is what helps me understand losing my legs.

A Nation Founded on Free Expression

The strength of our nation is found in its diversity. This strength was achieved through the exercise of our First Amendment right to freedom of expression—no matter how repugnant or offensive the expression might be. Achieving that strength has not been easy—it's been a struggle, a struggle lived by some very important men in my life and me.

In addition to my own military combat experience, I have been involved in veterans' affairs as a clinical social worker, program manager, board member, and advocate since 1974. I have yet to hear a veteran I have lived or worked with say that his/her service and sacrifice was in pursuit of protecting the flag. When confronted with the horrific demands of combat, most of us who are honest say we fought to stay alive. Combatants do not return home awestruck by the flag. Putting the pretty face of protecting the flag on the unforgettable, unspeakable, abominations of combat seems to trivialize what my fellow veterans and I experienced. . . .

I am offended when I see the flag burned or treated disrespectfully. As offensive and painful as this is, I still believe that those dissenting voices need to be heard. This country is unique and special because the minority, the unpopular, the dissenters and the downtrodden, also have a voice and are allowed to be heard in whatever way they choose to express themselves that does not harm others. Supporting freedom of expression, even when it hurts, is the truest test of our dedication to the belief that we have that right.

Importance of the Right to Dissent

Free expression, especially the right to dissent with the policies of the government, is one important element, if not the cornerstone of our form of government that has greatly enhanced its stability, prosperity, and strength of our country....

Freedom is what makes the United States of America strong and great, and freedom, including the right to dissent, is what has kept our democracy going for more than 200 years. And it is freedom that will continue to keep it strong for my children and the children of all the people like my father, late father in law, grandfather, brother, me, and others like us who served honorably and proudly for freedom.

No Exceptions to the First Amendment

Freedom cannot survive if exceptions to the First Amendment are made when someone in power disagrees with an expression. If we allow that, our right to free speech will depend on what Congress finds acceptable, precisely what the First Amendment was designed to prevent.

American Civil Liberties Union, March 4, 2004.

The pride and honor we feel is not in the flag per se. It's in the principles that it stands for and the people who have defended them. My pride and admiration is in our country, its people and its fundamental principles. I am grateful for the many heroes of our country—and especially those in my family. All the sacrifices of those who went before me would be for naught, if an amendment were added to the Constitution that cut back on our First Amendment rights for the first time in the history of our great nation.

I love this country, its people and what it stands for. The last thing I want to give the future generations are fewer rights than I was privileged to have. My family and I served and fought for others to have such freedoms and I am opposed to any actions which would restrict my children and their children from having the same freedoms I enjoy.

A Dangerous Amendment

The proposed amendment will apparently prohibit yet to be defined abuses of the flag which are deemed offensive. Who shall write the definition? Will destroying the flag in the interest of registering strong objection to a military excursion violate the law? What about reducing this revered icon to a lamp shade? Would the inclusion of a flag in a wall hanging violate the law? What if used as a curtain? Who decides?

If one peruses the pages of the periodicals of the traditional veterans' organizations, many of which apparently support this amendment, one will observe many uses of this revered symbol. Do those who object to a flag motif in clothing have recourse under the proposed amendment? If the flag can be worn on the uniform shoulder by safety and law enforcement personnel, is it permissible for it to be worn on underclothing? Who will check?

The proposal seems unenforceable. It raises the specter of the "flag police," whose duties would include searching out violations and bringing offenders to the bar of justice. That this is defended in the name of freedom and in the memory of valiant sacrifices by millions of this country's veterans is duplicitous and cynical. . . .

I respectfully submit that this assault on First Amendment freedoms in the name of protecting anything is incorrect and unjust. This amendment would create a chilling environment for political protest. The powerful anger which is elicited at the sight of flag burning is a measure of the love and respect most of us have for the flag.

Prohibiting this powerful symbolic discourse would stifle legitimate political dissent. If it is to be truly representative of our cherished freedoms, the flag itself must be available as a vehicle to express these freedoms.

This is among the freedoms for which I fought and gave part of my body. This is a part of the legacy I want to leave for my children. This is among the freedoms my grandfather was defending in WWI. It is among the freedoms my father and late father in law defended during their combat service during WWII.

*"Flag desecration is not speech, and it
desecrates our Constitution to say so."*

The Proposed Flag Protection Amendment Is Not a Threat to Liberty in America

Patrick H. Brady

Flag burning should not be categorized as free speech, argues Patrick H. Brady in the following viewpoint, which was originally given as congressional testimony on March 10, 2004. He supports an amendment to the U.S. Constitution that was proposed in 2004, which if passed, would outlaw flag desecration. According to Brady, this amendment does not threaten free speech. He contends that the majority of Americans believe that flag desecration should not be allowed, and that the Constitution should be amended to support this popular opinion. Brady is a retired major general in the U.S. Army.

As you read, consider the following questions:

1. How did James Madison and Thomas Jefferson, the framers of the Constitution, feel about flag burning, as cited by the author?
2. What does burning the flag teach, according to Brady?
3. What is the author's response to critics who say the flag is precious yet oppose protection?

Patrick H. Brady, testimony before the U.S. Senate Judiciary Committee, Washington, DC, March 10, 2004.

No matter how emotionally it affects most people, flag burning is a petty act, surely done to attract attention, to attack our country, our traditions and patriotism—but petty nonetheless. So I want to make it clear from the beginning that our primary concern is not flag-burners. They are with us always, along with others who hate America.

Our concern is the Constitution and those who have amended the Constitution—without the approval of the people, by inserting flag burning in the Bill of Rights—and others who would deny the people the right to decide this issue.[1]

This struggle for our flag has been long and fatiguing, but we are energized in this effort by our contract with patriotism, the oath we took to protect and defend our Constitution, an oath that defines patriotism. All Americans take this same oath when they recite the Pledge of Allegiance.

Flag Burning Is Not Speech

And that is the bottom line: by defending the right of the people to protect the flag, we are defending the Constitution. The Supreme Court made a mistake by calling flag burning "speech," and it is the duty of every American to correct any error by our government. Flag desecration is not speech, and it desecrates our Constitution to say so. A review of the magnitude of great Americans who support this fact confirms it.

Baseball great Tommy Lasorda spoke to common sense, the dictionary and for three of four common Americans when he said, "Speech is when you talk."

Justice Hugo Black spoke for every chief justice of the United States and justices on five Supreme Courts in the last century when he said, "It passes my belief that anything in the federal Constitution bars . . . making the deliberate burning of the American flag an offense."

U.S. Rep. John Murtha spoke for 70 percent of the Congress when he said, "Burning and destruction of the flag is

1. In 1989 the U.S. Supreme Court ruled that flag burning is a form of speech and thus protected by the First Amendment. However, many people argue that flag burning desecrates the Bill of Rights. There have been repeated attempts to pass an amendment that bans flag burning.

not speech. It is an act, an act that inflicts insult—insult that strikes at the very core of who we are as Americans and why so many of us fought, and many died, for this country."

Gen. Norman Schwarzkopf spoke for our warriors when he said, "I regard the legal protection of our flag as an absolute necessity and a matter of critical importance to our nation."

We have heard from opponents of the flag amendment that our troops fight for the rights of flag burners. Who among them would stand before these men and women and tell them they are fighting and dying on the streets of Iraq so that their flag can be burned on the streets of America?

Add to this mighty armada the legislatures of all 50 states and our president, and no reasonable person could deny that the court made a mistake.

James Madison, the author of the First Amendment, also condemned flag burning, as did [former U.S. president] Thomas Jefferson. The framers intended to protect political speech—the persuading power that moves people to the ballot box and those elected to the will of the people. Flag burning is the persuading power of the mobs.

What the communist Gregory Johnson said when he burned the flag—"Red, white and blue, we spit on you"—may not add to the political dialogue, but it is certainly protected by our Constitution. What he did—burning our flag—is not.

We could go on, but [author] Walter Berns said it very well in "Making Patriots" when he wrote, "The First Amendment protects freedom of speech, not expression, and, whereas all speech may be expression of a sort, not all expression is speech, and there is good reason why the framers of the First Amendment protected the one and not the other." The good reason is not difficult to see: the Constitution cannot pick and choose between actions that are speech and those that are not. Then, too, common sense tells us that if the framers meant expression, the protection of the press and assembly become redundant.

But legalized flag burning goes beyond desecration of our Constitution; it also desecrates our values as a nation. Burning the flag is wrong, but what it teaches is worse. It teaches that the outrageous conduct of a minority is more important than the will of the majority. It teaches that our laws need not reflect our values, and it teaches disrespect for the values embedded in our Constitution as embodied by our flag.

Yet, despite the enormity of evidence, we believe it is important to address the concerns of those who are confused or disagree on this issue, and we have done this in some detail.

Critics of the Amendment Are Wrong

First, there are those who have said flag burning is speech and should be protected by the Constitution but say they want a statute to protect the flag. The Supreme Court has made it clear that they will not allow a flag-protection statute. It has been tried.

It is important to know that the flag amendment [being proposed in 2004] does not protect the flag; it simply takes control of the flag away from the judges and returns it to the people, where they can protect it if they choose.[2]

Those who want a flag-protection law can have it simply by voting for the flag amendment. But how can those who say flag desecration is speech support a law forbidding flag desecration?

[Former] Secretary of State Colin Powell is often quoted by those who support legalized flag burning when he said, "I would not amend that great shield of democracy to hammer a few miscreants." Powell completely misses the point. Our goal is not to hammer miscreants who desecrate the flag; it is to hammer miscreants on the courts who desecrate the Constitution by calling flag-burning "speech." If we do not do so, we violate our oath to protect the Constitution and will soon have no shield of democracy.

To those who say the flag amendment would amend the Bill of Rights, we ask if the Supreme Court in 1989 had voted to protect the flag, would they then have amended the Bill of Rights?

To those who have difficulty defining the American flag and express concern over prosecuting people who burn biki-

---

2. As of the writing of this viewpoint, the amendment was still being debated in Congress.

nis embroidered with the flag or toilet paper marked with the flag, we ask if they would put toilet paper or a bikini on the coffin of a veteran, or their own coffin. For over 200 years we had laws defining flag desecration, and our courts had no problem defining a flag. Any fifth-grader knows the difference between a flag and a bikini.

To those who say the flag is precious to them but oppose protection, we ask if they have anything that they love or that is precious to them which they would not protect. Is there any other precious symbol in America that is not protected? Pat Boone said that was like saying, "I love my mother, but it is OK to bat her around."

A Neglible Impact on Speech

It turns out that the flag amendment would not limit freedom of speech very much at all. No words or beliefs would be prohibited; no opinions would be suppressed. A single manner of protest would be enjoined, but the ideas behind the protest could still be expressed in a multitude of ways. . . . Had the original First Amendment included a flag exception—"Congress shall make no law abridging the freedom of speech, except for flag burning"—there is little doubt that the subsequent history of popular democracy would have been entirely unaffected.

Stephen Lubet, *American Legion Magazine*, June 2004.

Some distrust the will of the majority, even fear a tyranny of the majority. They worry that the majority may exercise its will on a more virtuous minority. To them, we ask if the minority on the court who voted to protect the flag was more virtuous than the majority who voted for flag burners, or if the minority that voted for their opponent was more virtuous than the majority that voted for them.

Some have actually said that since dictators protect their flag, protecting our flag aligns us with dictators.

We wonder how any American can compare Old Glory, designed by the father of our country and protected according to the will of a free people, to the hammer and sickle or swastika, protected according to the will of a dictator.

Jefferson and Madison believed our flag should be protected. Does that align them with Stalin or Hitler?

The Constitution Should Be Amended

Some are concerned with the number of efforts to amend the Constitution. Why? Why is there no concern when the courts amend the Constitution? They do it frequently and illegally.

Why does the majority count only when it wears black robes and not when it wears working clothes? Look what the majority on courts has done with pornography, with prayer, with the Ten Commandments, with the Pledge, with the Boy Scouts and with marriage.

There have been more than 11,000 attempts to amend the Constitution, and only 27 have succeeded. The people take this responsibility very seriously.

An amendment that addresses the Bill of Rights could start a great debate and awaken the people to what is being done to their Constitution. Once the people are aware, they will be outraged, and they will act. We have seen their outrage after the Super Bowl and their impact on the moral midgets in the media. And we saw the people's outrage in California. They fired their governor, and that sent a message to all politicians.[3] We need to send a message to the courts.

The flag amendment will energize the people and could help stop the slippery slope of constitutional desecrations.

The Constitution is too important to be left to the courts, and so is the flag. They both belong to the people, and it is time for this body to let the people decide. If that flag is precious enough to cover the coffins of our dead warriors, it is precious enough to be protected.

3. After singer Janet Jackson exposed her breast at the 2004 Super Bowl, public outrage spurred an attempt to limit indecency in the media. In 2003 the people of California accused Governor Gray Davis of mismanagement, and voted to replace him.

Periodical Bibliography

The following articles have been selected to supplement the diverse views presented in this chapter.

Broadcasting & Cable   "Clear and Present Danger," March 22, 2004.

Business Week   "Oh Janet, What Hast Thou Wrought?" March 22, 2004.

Joseph Contreras   "Under-the-Radar Radio: While the FCC Cracks Down on Howard Stern, Hispanic Shock Jocks Are as Raunchy as Ever," *Newsweek*, May 3, 2004.

Howard Dean   "We Can Do Better," *Wall Street Journal*, August 22, 2003.

Fred Goodman   "The FCC Takes on Eminem," *Rolling Stone*, July 19, 2001.

David Hatch   "Media Ownership," *CQ Researcher*, October 10, 2003.

Marjorie Heins   "The Strange Case of Sarah Jones," *Censorship News*, Spring 2003.

Nat Hentoff   "First Amendment Treats for the Rich," *Village Voice*, January 21–27, 2004.

David Limbaugh   "Free Speech Must Be Protected," *Conservative Chronicle*, April 10, 2002.

Stephen Lubet   "Toward Purposeful Dissent," *American Legion Magazine*, June 2004.

Stephen J. Lyons   "Freedom of the Press Is Eroding Before Our Eyes," *High Country News*, November 11, 2002.

Bill Press   "Wal-Mart: Welcome to the New American Taliban," *Liberal Opinion Week*, July 7, 2003.

R.J. Samuelson   "Stranglehold on Speech," *Washington Post*, April 8, 2002.

Todd Shields   "Common Decency: As Powell's FCC Tries to Find the Middle Ground Between Censorship and First Amendment Rights, the Media Continue to Push the Envelope," *Mediaweek*, February 16, 2004.

Bradley Smith, Stuart Taylor, and John Samples   "Free Speech and Campaign Finance," *Cato Policy Report*, March/April 2004.

Jesse Walker   "Free Your Radio: Three Liberties We've Lost to the FCC," *Reason*, December 2001.

George Will   "First Amendment Is Being Abridged," *Conservative Chronicle*, July 3, 2002.

For Further Discussion

Chapter 1

1. The right to speak freely in the United States is protected by the First Amendment to the U.S. Constitution, which states: "Congress shall make no law . . . abridging the freedom of speech." However, Jonah Goldberg argues that some speech must be censored in order to protect members of society. The American Civil Liberties Union contends that even unpopular speech should be allowed. In your view, which author is most convincing? Why?

2. Kevin W. Saunders argues that children do not deserve the same First Amendment protection as adults, and that some censorship is necessary for their protection. Charles Taylor believes that it is unnecessary and often harmful to censor public expression for the protection of children. Based on your reading of the viewpoints, should the First Amendment apply differently to children than to adults? Why or why not?

3. The press plays an important part in U.S. democracy by keeping the public informed about current events, and its freedom is specifically protected by the First Amendment. Anthony Lewis argues that the press should never be censored, especially during times of crisis. Carlos A. Kelly contends that during a crisis, press self-censorship is often necessary. Do you believe that the press should engage in self-censorship during times of crisis such as the war on terrorism? Why or why not? Is press censorship ever justified during times of peace, in your opinion? Explain.

4. Both David Ebel and Rodney Smolla believe the right to privacy in one's home should be protected. However, while Ebel believes that this right includes freedom from telemarketers, Smolla argues that telemarketers' right to free speech is more important than individual privacy. In your opinion, how should the right to free speech be balanced with the right of individual privacy? Do you believe the National Do Not Call Registry is constitutional? Cite from the text to support your answer.

Chapter 2

1. Both children and adults use library computers to access the Internet. William H. Rehnquist supports the Supreme Court's 2003 decision that in order to protect children, libraries that receive federal funding must install Internet filters on their computers. Clarence Page argues that these filters do not work and

violate the rights of adults to view whatever Internet content they wish. Which author offers a more persuasive argument? Why? How do you think libraries should balance the rights of children and adults to use the Internet?

2. According to J. Robert Flores, Internet pornography can, and should, be censored by the government. Eugene Volokh contends that this is impossible. Do you think the U.S. government can successfully reduce pornography on the Internet? What might be the effects of such government regulation?

3. Charles E. Schumer contends that spam is a threat to the Internet and consumers, and must be reduced through regulation. Clyde Wayne Crews Jr. agrees that spam is often undesirable, however he argues that the government should not regulate it. How does Crews believe the spam problem can be solved? How does his solution differ from Schumer's? Which argument do you find more convincing and why?

Chapter 3

1. The Patriot Act gives the government increased powers to fight the war against terrorism. Eleanor J. Bader argues that these powers constitute a violation of Americans' right to free expression. John Ashcroft contends that claims such as this are unfounded. After reading these two arguments, do you believe that the Patriot Act has caused increased censorship in the United States? Why or why not?

2. Both Simon Houpt and Bobby Eberle discuss the way some people have expressed criticism of America's war on terrorism. These two authors, however, offer different interpretations of the way dissenters have been treated in the United States. What does Houpt believe has happened to dissenters in America? How do you think Eberle would respond to Houpt's argument?

3. Alex Gourevitch maintains that the Iraqi media have been censored under the U.S. occupation of that country. Ilene R. Prusher contends that under the occupation, the Iraqi media are more free than ever before. After reading these two viewpoints, what obstacles do you think exist to media freedom in Iraq? Do you believe the Iraqi media are more free under U.S. occupation? Why or why not?

Chapter 4

1. Adam Thierer asserts that government censorship of broadcast media is unnecessary and harmful to society. Jonathan S. Adelstein contends that because the media refuse to regulate crude and offensive content, the government must step in and enforce

broadcast standards. Do you believe that government regulation is necessary, or should individuals decide what media content they are exposed to? Cite the authors to support your answer.

2. Gene Kimmelman and Michael K. Powell both advance the claim that media diversity is an important part of democracy in the United States. According to Powell, this diversity exists in the U.S. media; however, Kimmelman argues that this is not the case. In your opinion, which author is more convincing? Please explain, citing from the viewpoints.

3. Gary E. May believes that flag burning is a form of speech, and that banning it would be unconstitutional. Patrick H. Brady contends that flag burning is not speech and does not deserve constitutional protection. In your opinion, is flag burning a form of speech? Why or why not? Do you believe that Congress should pass an amendment banning flag desecration? Explain.

Organizations to Contact

The editors have compiled the following list of organizations concerned with the issues debated in this book. The descriptions are derived from materials provided by the organizations. All have publications or information available for interested readers. The list was compiled on the date of publication of the present volume; names, addresses, phone and fax numbers, and e-mail addresses may change. Be aware that many organizations take several weeks or longer to respond to inquiries, so allow as much time as possible.

American Civil Liberties Union (ACLU)
125 Broad St., Eighteenth Floor, New York, NY 10004
(212) 549-2500 • fax: (212) 549-2646
e-mail: aclu@aclu.org • Web site: www.aclu.org

The ACLU is a national organization that defends Americans' civil rights. It adamantly opposes regulation of all forms of speech, including pornography and hate speech. The ACLU offers numerous reports, fact sheets, and policy statements on a wide variety of issues. Publications include the briefing papers "Freedom of Expression," "Hate Speech on Campus," and "Popular Music Under Siege."

American Library Association (ALA)
50 E. Huron St., Chicago, IL 60611
(800) 545-2433 • fax: (312) 440-9347
e-mail: ala@ala.org • Web site: www.ala.org

The ALA is the nation's primary professional organization for librarians. Through its Office for Intellectual Freedom (OIF), the ALA supports free access to libraries and library materials. The OIF also monitors and opposes efforts to ban books. The ALA's sister organization, the Freedom to Read Foundation, provides legal defense for libraries. Publications of the ALA include the *Newsletter on Intellectual Freedom*, articles, fact sheets, and policy statements, including "Protecting the Freedom to Read."

Canadian Association for Free Expression (CAFE)
PO Box 332, Station B, Etobicoke, ON M9W 5L3 Canada
(905) 897-7221
e-mail: cafe@canadafirst.net
Web site: www.canadianfreespeech.com

CAFE, one of Canada's leading civil liberties groups, works to strengthen the freedom of speech and freedom of expression provisions in the Canadian Charter of Rights and Freedoms. It lobbies politicians and researches threats to freedom of speech. Publications include specialized reports, leaflets, and the *Free Speech Monitor*, which is published ten times per year.

Cato Institute
1000 Massachusetts Ave. NW, Washington, DC 20001
(202) 842-0200 • fax: (202) 842-3490
e-mail: cato@cato.org • Web site: www.cato.org
The Cato Institute is a libertarian public policy research foundation dedicated to limiting the role of government and promoting individual liberty. The institute publishes the quarterly magazine *Regulation*, the bimonthly *Cato Policy Report*, and numerous papers dealing with censorship, including "Sex, Cyberspace, and the First Amendment," and "Titillating TV and Creeping Censorship."

Center for Constitutional Rights (CCR)
666 Broadway, Seventh Floor, New York, NY 10012
(212) 614-6464 • fax: (212) 614-6499
Web site: www.ccr-ny.org
CCR is a nonprofit legal and educational organization dedicated to protecting and advancing the rights guaranteed by the U.S. Constitution and the Universal Declaration of Human Rights. The organization uses litigation to empower minority and poor communities and to strengthen the broader movement for constitutional and human rights. It opposes the government's use of censorship since the September 11, 2001, terrorist attacks. CCR publishes books, pamphlets, fact sheets, and reports, such as *The State of Civil Liberties: One Year Later.*

Electronic Frontier Foundation (EFF)
1550 Bryant St., Suite 725, San Francisco, CA 94103
(415) 436-9333 • fax: (415) 436-9993
e-mail: ask@eff.org • Web site: www.eff.org
EFF is a nonprofit, nonpartisan organization that works to protect privacy and freedom of expression in the arena of computers and the Internet. Its missions include supporting litigation that protects First Amendment rights. EFF's Web site publishes an electronic bulletin, *Effector*, and the guidebook *Protecting Yourself Online: The Definitive Resource on Safety, Freedom, and Privacy in Cyberspace.*

Family Research Council (FRC)
700 Thirteenth St. NW, Suite 500, Washington, DC 20005
(202) 393-2100 • fax: (202) 393-2134
e-mail: corrdept@frc.org • Web site: www.frc.org

The Family Research Council is an organization that believes pornography degrades women and children and seeks to strengthen current obscenity laws. It publishes the monthly newsletter *Washington Watch* and the bimonthly journal *Family Policy*, which features a full-length essay in each issue, such as "Keeping Libraries User and Family Friendly: The Challenge of Internet Pornography." The FRC also publishes policy papers, including "Indecent Proposal: The NEA Since the Supreme Court Decency Decision," and "Internet Filtering and Blocking Technology."

Freedom Forum
1101 Wilson Blvd., Arlington, VA 22209
(703) 528-0800 • fax: (703) 284-2836
e-mail: news@freedomforum.org
Web site: www.freedomforum.org

The Freedom Forum is an international organization that works to protect freedom of the press and free speech. It monitors developments in media and First Amendment issues on its Web site, in its monthly magazine *Forum News*, and in the *Media Studies Journal*, published twice a year.

Free Speech Coalition
PO Box 10480, Canoga Park, CA 91309
(800) 845-8503 • (818) 348-9373
e-mail: freespeech@pacificnet.net
Web site: www.freespeechcoalition.com

The Free Speech Coalition is a trade association that represents members of the adult entertainment industry. It seeks to protect the industry from attempts to censor pornography. Publications include the report *The Truth About the Adult Entertainment Industry.*

International Freedom of Expression Exchange (IFEX)
IFEX Clearing House
489 College St., Suite 403, Toronto, ON M6G 1A5 Canada
(416) 515-9622 • fax: (416) 515-7879
e-mail: ifex@ifex.org • Web site: www.ifex.org

IFEX consists of more than forty organizations that support freedom of expression. Its work is coordinated by the Toronto-based Clearing House. Through the Action Alert Network, organizations report abuses of free expression to the Clearing House, which distributes the information throughout the world. Publications include the weekly *Communiqué*, which reports on free expression triumphs and violations.

Morality in Media (MIM)
475 Riverside Dr., Suite 239, New York, NY 10115
(212) 870-3222 • fax: (212) 870-2765
e-mail: mim@moralitymedia.org
Web site: www.moralitymedia.org

Morality in Media is an interfaith organization that fights obscenity and opposes indecency in the mainstream media. It believes pornography harms society and maintains the National Obscenity Law Center, a clearinghouse of materials on obscenity law. Publications include the bimonthlies *Morality in Media* and *Obscenity Law Bulletin*, and reports, including "Pornography's Effects on Adults and Children."

National Coalition Against Censorship (NCAC)
275 Seventh Ave., New York, NY 10001
(212) 807-6222 • fax: (212) 807-6245
e-mail: ncac@ncac.org • Web site: www.ncac.org

The NCAC represents more than forty national organizations that work to prevent suppression of free speech and the press. It educates the public about the dangers of censorship and how to oppose it. The coalition publishes *Censorship News* five times a year, articles, various reports, and background papers. Papers include "Censorship's Tool Du Jour: V-Chips, TV Ratings, PICS, and Internet Filters."

National Coalition for the Protection of Children & Families
800 Compton Rd., Suite 9224, Cincinnati, OH 45231-9964
(513) 521-6227 • fax: (513) 521-6337
Web site: www.nationalcoalition.org

The coalition is an organization of business, religious, and civic leaders who work to eliminate pornography. It encourages citizens to support the enforcement of obscenity laws and to close down neighborhood pornography outlets. Publications include the books *Final Report of the Attorney General's Commission on Pornography*, *The Mind Polluters*, and *Pornography: A Human Tragedy*.

People for the American Way (PFAW)
2000 M St. NW, Suite 400, Washington, DC 20036
(202) 467-4999 • fax: (202) 293-2672
e-mail: pfaw@pfaw.org • Web site: www.pfaw.org

PFAW works to promote citizen participation in democracy and safeguard the principles of the U.S. Constitution, including the right to free speech. It publishes a variety of fact sheets, articles, and position statements on its Web site and distributes the e-mail newsletter *Freedom to Learn Online*.

Bibliography of Books

Steve Allen — *Vulgarians at the Gate: Trash TV and Raunch Radio: Raising the Standards of Popular Culture.* Amherst, NY: Prometheus, 2001.

Martin Barker and Julian Petley, eds. — *Ill Effects: The Media/Violence Debate.* New York: Routledge, 2001.

Tammy Bruce — *The New Thought Police: Inside the Left's Assault on Free Speech and Free Minds.* Roseville, CA: Forum, 2001.

Simone Chambers and Anne Costain, eds. — *Deliberation, Democracy, and the Media.* Lanham, MD: Rowman & Littlefield, 2000.

Katharine Gelber — *Speaking Back: The Free Speech Versus Hate Speech Debate.* Philadelphia: J. Benjamins, 2002.

Martin P. Golding — *Free Speech on Campus.* Lanham, MD: Rowman & Littlefield, 2000.

Marjorie Heins — *Not in Front of the Children: "Indecency," Censorship and the Innocence of Youth.* New York: Hill and Wang, 2001.

Thomas R. Hensley, ed. — *The Boundaries of Freedom of Expression and Order in American Democracy.* Kent, OH: Kent State University Press, 2001.

Philip Jenkins — *Beyond Tolerance: Child Pornography on the Internet.* New York: New York University Press, 2001.

Russ Kick, ed. — *Abuse Your Illusions: The Disinformation Guide to Media Mirages and Establishment Lies.* New York: Disinformation, 2003.

Rebecca Knuth — *Libricide: The Regime-Sponsored Destruction of Books and Libraries in the Twentieth Century.* Westport, CT: Praeger, 2003.

Judith Levine — *Harmful to Minors: The Perils of Protecting Children from Sex.* Minneapolis: University of Minnesota Press, 2002.

Jeremy Harris Lipschultz — *Free Expression in the Age of the Internet: Social and Legal Boundaries.* Boulder, CO: Westview, 2000.

Pippa Norris, Montague Kern, and Marion Just, eds. — *Framing Terrorism: The News Media, the Government, and the Public.* New York: Routledge, 2003.

Robert S. Peck — *Libraries, the First Amendment, and Cyberspace: What You Need to Know.* Chicago: American Library Association, 2000.

Peter Philips   *Censored 2003: The Top 25 Censored Stories.* New York: Seven Stories, 2002.

Monroe E. Price and Stefaan G. Verhulst, eds.   *Parental Control of Television Broadcasting.* Mahwah, NJ: Lawrence Erlbaum, 2002.

Diane Ravitch   *The Language Police: How Pressure Groups Restrict What Children Learn.* New York: Knopf, 2003.

David L. Robb   *Operation Hollywood: How the Pentagon Shapes and Censors the Movies.* Amherst, NY: Prometheus, 2004.

Lawrence C. Soley   *Censorship, Inc.: The Corporate Threat to Free Speech in the United States.* New York: Monthly Review, 2002.

May Taylor and Ethel Quayle   *Child Pornography: An Internet Crime.* New York: Brunner-Routledge, 2003.

Alexander Tsesis   *Destructive Messages: How Hate Speech Paves the Way for Harmful Social Movements.* New York: New York University Press, 2002.

John F. Wirenius   *First Amendment, First Principles: Verbal Acts and Freedom of Expression.* New York: Holmes, 2000.

Index

192